# Apostolic Manifesto

## By Dr. Ernest Maddox

TO: Rev. Daniel R. Jarrett

From Dr. Maddox

5/23/15

# Apostolic Manifesto

Dr. E. Maddox Ministries
P.O. Box 48547 Oak Park, MI. 48237
www.dremaddox.org
dr.ernest.maddox@gmail.com
Phone 248-796-8523

Paper Back ISBN 978-0-9779748-3-2
E-Book 978-0-9779748-4-9

# Apostolic Manifesto

# Table of Contents

# Table of Contents

# Table of Contents

# Apostolic Manifesto

# Dedication

This book is dedicated to those who sense, know, and have experienced the abuse of churches and ministries that are not legitimately bound to Jesus Christ. To church leaders who have sought change that would bring them closer to Jesus Christ, but found themselves ridiculed and excommunicated. For those who have prayed that Jesus Christ, would regain the Lordship of the Christian activity that he shed his blood for.

This book is dedicated to those who are prepared to shed the garments of "Religious Theology" and move into true God Theocracy. This book is dedicated to those who have been prepared and are ready to wage legitimate Spiritual Warfare. This book is dedicated to those who have been equipped and are ready to cast Satan not just out of people, but out of The Church of the living God.

This book is dedicated to those legitimate Christian men and women around the world who are ready to carry out the legitimate great commission of The Church. This book is dedicated to eliminating hybrid compromise, and paganism embedded in so called Christianity.

*Mar 16:15 And he said unto them, Go ye into all the world, and preach the gospel to every creature. Mar 16:16 He that believeth and is baptized shall be saved; but he that believeth not shall be damned. Mar 16:17 And these signs shall follow them that believe; In my name shall they cast out devils; they shall speak with new tongues Mar16:18 They shall take up serpents; and if they drink any deadly thing, it shall not hurt them; they*

# Dedication

*shall lay hands on the sick, and they shall recover. (KJV)*

Finally, this book is dedicated to everyone that is vexed by the many abominations being committed in The Church. Those who choose to have **S.W.A.G.G.**, (Standing-Staying With A Great God), the "Holy Triune God."

> *Eze 9:4 And the LORD said unto him, Go through the midst of the city, through the midst of Jerusalem, and set a mark upon the foreheads of the men that sigh and that cry for all the abominations that be done in the midst thereof. (KJV)*

This book is an indictment against those who choose to **S.S.A.G.**, (Satanically Standing Against God), the "Holy Triune God." The "Holy Triune God", being the Father, Jesus Christ, and the Holy Spirit. Review Revelation 12:7-9 and 2 Corinthians 11:13-15, for some insight on the spirit behind **S.S.A.G.**, and how it operates. It is an antichrist spirit; see 1 John 2:18-26.

> *Eze 9:5 And to the others he said in mine hearing, Go ye after him through the city, and smite: let not your eye spare, neither have ye pity: Eze 9:6 Slay utterly old [and] young, both maids, and little children, and women: but come not near any man upon whom [is] the mark; and begin at my sanctuary. Then they began at the ancient men which [were] before the house. (KJV)*

# Dedication

For a partial list of "Abominations", see Deuteronomy 18:9-12, Proverbs 6:16-19, Romans 1:24-32, 1 Corinthians 6:9-10, Galatians 5:19-21, and Revelation 21:7-8.

Apostolic Manifesto

# **Preface**

The preparation for this book began in August, 1969, when I was baptized in the Father, Son, and the Holy Spirit. I was a young man from the streets twenty one years old. Simply stated I was a drug dealer and a gang banger. I thought that was life before I found Jesus Christ. I guess for many that would have been the case. However for me the true gang banging (spiritual warfare) had just begun. What I'm trying to say is that I thought church would be a place where I would not need my gang banging mentality or my drug dealer instinct. I soon came to realize how wrong I was.

I soon came to realize that racism, classism, economical division and social class discrimination, were and is more prominent in The Church than anything I had experienced growing up in the civil rights age. Actually, I coined a phrase to sum up the whole experience, "Spiritual Apartheid." I was in that environment for about thirty one years, where I had an opportunity to serve, with my wife, as social activities coordinator, district youth coordinator, youth pastor, and as an ordained leader of the local congregation.

God did this in spite of the extreme racism, abusive pastors, and many members who were highly intimidated and brain washed. African-Americans were led to believe that they were second-class Christians, and others were dehumanized. Educational elitism was praised, I would even say worshipped. I prayed to God, and asked Him, "Why did you send me here"? His response was, "I want to teach you what not to do. I want to show you that basically what you did in the

# Preface

name of gang banging, and drug dealing (in this church and many others) they do the same thing in the name of the gospel of Jesus Christ."

At the time those words were spoken to me I had a sixth grade education, and did not understand exactly what the Lord was saying. But the Lord indicated to me, "I will train and teach you for three decades." I didn't even know what the word decade meant, I had to look it up and when I realized a decade was ten years, I was not happy. I will just simply say that God kept his promise. Over that thirty one year period I earned a Bachelor's degree, two Masters Degrees, and one Doctorate degree. Eventually I would earn two more Doctorate degrees, for a total of six earned degrees.

In over forty four years of experience with church dynamics, relative to leadership, as well as so-called laity, along with a powerful insight of the Holy Spirit; I have developed a degree of insight. I have over thirty years as a consultant, trainer, and innovator in the church as well as in the secular arena. Because of that, I know it's time for this book, and that I am more than qualified to write it. I have provided additional information about my background and experience, in a short bio at the end of this book. I will do what the Father, the Son and the Holy Spirit, has prepared me for, and directed me to do. May God bless you, Amen.

# Apostolic Manifesto

# Introduction

The Church has changed drastically in the last fifty years relative to the foundations of Bible based Christianity. The Christian Church has lost ground to religions and ideologies of the secular world. There is an Anti-Christ spirit at work.

*We live in changing times-new churches are born as old ones die; new evangelistic methods emerge as old ones become ineffective; new worship expressions take center stage as old ones become empty traditions. The focus ... is to consider this time for new denominations as old ones collapse. Some Christians are frightened by changing times-they are threatened because of time changes for church meetings, or a change to a new Bible version, or a canceled program. When their denominations collapse around them, some people despair. Is it because their denominations propped up their faith, or maybe their whole lives were attached to their denomination, and when it deflated so did their Christianity?*

*America is moving into post modernism-a time when the Church no longer drives culture, nor does the Church have much influence on Society. Our culture is going beyond its past Christian influence to the neutralization of Christianity. We have become open to all religions; and at times our culture seems to be anti-Christian. (Wagner, 1998, p.7-8)*

One of the alternatives has been to form ecumenical-para church and ministry organizations. This has gone the way of denominations because the leadership tried to turn the organization into a religious

# Introduction

denomination. The same satanic/demonic trap that destroyed and is destroying denominations, is doing the same to the para church and ministry organizations.

God in the form of Jesus Christ is moving with an Apostolic Manifesto in Twenty-Thirteen (2013). The Church, ecumenical para church and ministry organizations are going to have to submit to the "Apostolic Manifesto" (Mandate). **That mandate is to put religion out of The Church and ministries and put Jesus Christ back in.**

The Church needs to get back to holiness in obedience, praise, worship, serving, giving, and respect for the broken body and shed blood of Jesus Christ. Holiness must be part of the administrative as well as the business aspect of what we do in the House of the One True God. We must get back to the proper understanding of Grace and teach it. The Church of the One True God must be re-aligned and allied with the One True Word of God. The One True God is the Father of creation and His Son is Jesus Christ. The One True Word is the Holy Bible, and the agent is the Holy Spirit.

The legitimate Apostle of today, must preach and teach the legitimate Word of the Creator God; with love and without compromise. Jesus established leadership in The Church. The Church should honor that.

*Eph 4:11 And he gave some, apostles; and some, prophets; and some, evangelists; and some, pastors and teachers; Eph 4:12 For the perfecting of the saints, for the work of the ministry, for the edifying of the body of Christ.*

# Introduction

*1Tim. 4:1 Now the Spirit speaketh expressly, that in the latter times some shall depart from the faith, giving heed to seducing spirits, and doctrines of devils;*

*1Tim 4:2 Speaking lies in hypocrisy; having their conscience seared with a hot iron;: 2Tim 4:1 I charge [thee] therefore before God, and the Lord Jesus Christ, who shall judge the quick and the dead at his appearing and his kingdom; 2Tim 4:2 Preach the word; be instant in season, out of season; reprove, rebuke, exhort with all longsuffering and doctrine. (KJV)*

Those of us with an Apostolic mantle must stand up and represent the Word of the Living God and declare His Holiness and His Greatness. The Creator God has set the Apostles first in the order of leadership, the Prophets have been placed second; (1Corinthians 12:28). They have the responsibility for alignment: correction, redirection, impartation, revelation, and leading the Bride of Christ to the marriage ceremony without blemish, spot, accusation or complaint.

# Apostolic Manifesto

# -1-

# The Backdrop

## *The Awakening*

God is moving in the spirit of the Apostolic, which is different from what has been done in a traditional church- ministry denomination paradigm.

> *The direction of world events has made a sharp turn. Before the mid-1980s, Christians were growing about 2% a year, barely above the world population growth rate. Now God has stormed onto the scene like a tornado. Compare today's annual growth rates:"*

> *Not only are core aposiolics growing far faster than Muslims, Hindus, Buddhists, and new agers, but in fair and even encounters, spiritual power prevails and Jesus wins perhaps 99% of the time. The main defenses of other religionists are not theological arguments, but violence, persecution, legal barriers, and propagandistic falsehoods.*

> *Core apostolic are the new saints who are at the heart of the mushrooming kingdom of God. The term and the category are both mine, but they're not at all subjective. They stand for a very real and countable movement of more than 707million switched-on disciples. The growth rate of Christians in general are so terribly low that they had clouded the picture, hiding the white-hot growth of the core apostolics. (Rutz, 2005, p.14)*

1

# -1-

# The Backdrop

## *Who/What are Apostles?*

In order to understand what it means to have an Apostolic Manifesto we must first understand what the concept of an Apostle really means. We must define what that term actually stands for and represents. First, we will examine a dictionary definition from Merriam-Webster's online dictionary. Defining the term Apostle will assist in the backdrop of reviewing the impact of that role.

### *Definition of Apostle*

*1: one sent on a mission: as a: one of an authoritative New Testament group sent out to preach the gospel and made up especially of Christ's 12 original disciples and Paul b: the first prominent Christian missionary to a region or group 2 a: a person who initiates a great moral reform or who first advocates an important belief or system b: an ardent supporter: adherent 3: the highest ecclesiastical official in some church organizations.*

*Synonyms: advocate, advocator, exponent, backer, booster, champion, expounder, espouser, friend, gospeler, high priest, paladin, promoter, proponent, protagonist, supporter, true believer, tub-thumper, white knight. Antonyms: adversary, antagonist, opponent Related Words: loyalist, partisan, stalwart; adherent, cohort, disciple, follower; interpreter; applauder, cheerleader, encourager, fellow traveler. Antonyms: enemy, foe, rival; belittler, critic, faultfinder. (Merriam-Webster)*

# -1-

# The Backdrop

It is important to look at the aspect of the Apostle from a thorough definition perspective. This will help us to understand the impact on and the perception of others relative to the Apostolic role, and what we must be concerned about in this apostolic era. We are looking at an Apostolic paradigm shift relative to leadership in the body of Christ Jesus.

### *Apostle are Called by God*

Apostles were not chosen by men but are ordained and called of God, therefore they have no allegiance to an organization nor an individual only to the throne of God. *Mark 3:13 "And he goeth up into a mountain, and calleth [unto him] whom he would: and they came unto him;" see verse14-18 for the who. Galatians 1:1 "Paul, an apostle, (not of men, neither by man, but by Jesus Christ, and God the Father, who raised him from the dead.)"* Legitimate apostles are tried, tested and purged. They have to prove themselves before the throne of God, that they are faithful and committed to the kingdom purpose.

When the definitions, synonyms, and antonyms of the word Apostle are examined you see a tremendous dynamic, of a force for change: emotion, commitment, with engagement are identified. You can identify the traits of a personality that causes change, that innovates, that is efficient and can move forward without a great deal of encouragement or agreement. Apostles understand the mission is for God, we need to recognize that in this twenty first century.

# -1-

# The Backdrop

## *Apostles Cause Conflict at the Gates of Hell*

Apostles have been called to change and restore. The original twelve disciples/apostles brought about a change in traditional religious practices in fact they restored the principles of God that had been in existence for eternity. This ideology God shared with the angels and then eventually with Adam and Eve. Disruption and destruction came about because of Satan's rebellion. When God introduced Adam and Eve into the garden, the serpent, a representation of Satan, again created havoc. For the last 6000 years there has been a back-and-forth battle of restoration, correction, re-establishing, and erecting the Kingdom of God.

The Apostolic Manifesto with prophetic partnership equals end time leadership; this is the mechanism of implementation. Apostles are the chief correctors of the body of Christ and are responsible for aligning the body of Christ Jesus with the Word of God; without regard for political correctness, religious protocol, new standards of moral behavior and social acceptance.

Denominations have robbed The Church (not the person of Christ Jesus) of its power, revelation, understanding, and the willingness to confront abominable behavior, outlined in the Holy texts. "The whole Earth is groaning for the manifestations of the sons of God"; see Romans the eighth chapter. The Apostolic resurrection is erupting and cannot be stopped, squashed, diminished, dismissed, or denied.

# Apostolic Manifesto

# -2-

# History of Conflict

## Pre Adam and Eve- First Point of Attack

I want to establish some foundational ground work. Let's turn to Isaiah the fourteenth chapter, and again we are laying the foundation because there is no point in discussing the aspects of the Apostolic Manifesto without discussing the aspects of spiritual warfare. Satan is the instigator and initiator of spiritual warfare. In Isaiah the fourteenth chapter, beginning in verse twelve, it states:

> *Isa 14:12 "How you are fallen from heaven, O Lucifer,\* son of the morning! [How] you are cut down to the ground, you who weakened the nations! Isa 14:13 For you have said in your heart: 'I will ascend into heaven, I will exalt my throne above the stars of God; I will also sit on the mount of the congregation On the farthest sides of the north; Isa 14:14 I will ascend above the heights of the clouds, I will be like the Most High. Isa 14:15 Yet you shall be brought down to Sheol, to the lowest depths of the Pit. (NKJV)*

Satan wanted to be like God. He wanted to usurp God's authority. Let's turn to Ezekiel 28, because again it describes the behavior of a being that is not human, but super natural.

> *Ezekiel 28:11 Moreover the word of the Lord came to me, saying, Eze. 28:12 Son of man, take up a lamentation for the king of Tyre, and say to him, 'Thus says the Lord God: (NKJV)*

# -2-

# History of Conflict

Relative to the King of Tyre, this proves that territorial demons and principalities rule in the physical affairs of men. As we move forward you will soon become aware that we are not talking about a physical being here, It says: *"You were the seal of perfection, Full of wisdom and perfect in beauty."* And that's no description of any human being we know. "*You were in Eden, the Garden of God."* So we know the King of Tyre was not in the Garden of Eden in the flesh. God is now speaking spiritually here.

Let's continue in Ezekiel 28:13; *"Every precious stone was your covering,"* and they are named. Going down to verse 14 it says; *"You were the anointed cherub who covers;"* It becomes clearer and clearer who God is talking about. It says, *"I established you; You were on the holy mountain of God. You walked back and forth in the midst of fiery stones."*

No human being is capable of doing that. I know some people say, "Well, I have seen individuals walk on hot coals." This was a great deal more than hot coals; this was fiery stones. It says, *"You were perfect in your Ways from the day you were created, till iniquity was found in you." "By the abundance of your trading you became filled with violence within. And you sinned."* So Satan sinned and his main sin was pride. And it says: "*Therefore I cast you as a profane thing out of the mountain of God."* Which means the Kingdom of God, or the domain of God. *"And I (God) destroyed you, covering cherub, from the midst of the fiery stones." (Ezekiel 28: 15-16 NKLV)*

# -2-

# History of Conflict

In other words, he was removed from his position of loftiness. His job was to be a "light bringer" to God's creation, he was Lucifer. That was his job description before he became Satan. As we have already noted in Isaiah 14 and Ezekiel 28, he was in a prominent position until he decided to rebel. Now this happened long before the creation of Adam and Eve. In this section I want to bring this into a context in Genesis that few have truly understood. Many have read, and too many have misunderstood. The events of Isaiah 14 and Ezekiel 28; Genesis 1:1 and Genesis 1:2.

### *Post Adam and Eve-Second Point of Attack*

Let's go to Genesis the first chapter, and in the first verse. It says, **"*In the beginning God created the heavens and the earth.*** Now in verse two it says, ***"The earth was without form."*** Like in New King James a lot of English translations give the impression that God created the Earth in chaos. This is not the case. When you look up that particular verse in the Hebrew, verse two reads more in the context of *"the earth became void and without form."* The Hebrew words there are *tohu* and *bohu,* which means it was a condition that became chaotic after the events in verse one. What happened between verses one and verses two, is stated in Isaiah 14:12-17, and Ezekiel 28:1-19. I recommend that you do more research on what happened.

These events happened after the creation of perfection, because Lucifer, who became Satan, was created in perfection. Why would God create him "in perfection", as says in Ezekiel, and

# -2-

# History of Conflict

then create the Earth in imperfection? It became that way because of the battle that occurred in Isaiah 14 and Ezekiel 28. When you understand the Hebrew meaning of the words and the timeline, it becomes very clear that the imperfection became extant between the events in verse one and verse two of Genesis one.

As you read the Scriptures, you can see the reality of Satan's impact and what he eventually did in the way of destruction and total chaos. In John 10:10 it says, *"The thief cometh not, but for to steal, and to kill, and to destroy:"* This is what Lucifer became between verses one and two of Genesis the first chapter. What time expired between those two events? The timeline is not identified in scriptures. Now, why is the event important?

As we move to Genesis, the third chapter we can see that this pre-Adamic conflict is now brought to the Adamic realm (Adam/Eve's realm). Let us move from the heavenly battle as identified in Revelation, Isaiah, Ezekiel, and Genesis, to where that battle is now reduced to the Earth.

When we look at Genesis 3:1 it says, now the serpent (who used to be Lucifer). *"Now the serpent was more cunning than any beast of the field which the Lord God had made."* One of the meanings for serpent in Hebrew is "enchanter". So when you think of serpent don't think of something just crawling but think of something with great persuasive power. *"And he [the serpent] said to the woman, Has God indeed said, 'You shall not eat of every tree of the garden'?"*

# -2-

# History of Conflict

Now we see the enemy, Satan, trying to bring his insurrection, his attitude of rebellion, and his sin to the realm of mankind. Genesis 2:9. *"And out of the ground the Lord God made every tree grow."* And it says, *"In the midst of the garden there was the tree or trees that were good and pleasant and the tree of life was also in the midst"* (I am paraphrasing) *"of the garden and the tree of the knowledge of good and evil."* Genesis 2:16, *"And the Lord God commanded the man saying, of every tree of the garden you may freely eat, every tree but one. But of the tree (verse 17) of the Knowledge of Good and Evil you shall not eat, for in the day that you eat of it you shall surely die. "*Now, let's move back to Genesis 3:1-3 because you need to understand the subtlety in which the enemy operates:

> *"Now the serpent was more cunning than any beast of the field which the Lord God had made. And he said to the woman, Has God indeed said, 'You shall not eat of every tree of the garden'?" And the woman said to the serpent, we may eat the fruit of the trees of the garden; but of the fruit of the tree which is in the midst of the garden, God has said, 'You shall not eat of it, nor shall you touch it, lest you die." (NKJV)*

In the instructions God gave to Adam, we don't see anything about touching. According to Eve's response, she said that "we could not eat of any tree that was in the midst of the garden." The tree of life was in the midst of the garden, they had permission to eat from that tree. Eve's response was not exactly correct, which

# -2-

# History of Conflict

goes to Adam's dissemination of information. The key here is that the enemy wanted to taint the instructions of God.

Then the serpent said to the woman, *"You will not surely die."* Genesis 3:4, God says *"Thou shall surely die."* Notice the level of warfare and the subtlety that Satan uses by adding the word *"not."* He took the truth and perverted it. Satan goes on to say in verse 5, *"For God knows that in the day you eat of it your eyes will be opened, and you will be like God, knowing good and evil."* So when the woman saw that the tree was good for food and a tree desirable to make one wise, she took of it.

> *Gen 3:6 So when the woman saw that the tree was good for food, that it was pleasant to the eyes, and a tree desirable to make one wise, she took of its fruit and ate. She also gave to her husband with her, and he ate. (NKJV)*

Adam was present when this occurred, he was not far away. The Word does not say she ran and gave it to him but, *"gave to her husband with her and he ate."* Genesis 3:7 *"Then the eyes of both of them were opened, and they knew that they were naked; and they sewed fig leaves together and made themselves coverings."*

Once this occurred, they became somewhat concerned because they were naked. But in Genesis 2:24-25; it says, *"Therefore a man shall leave his father and mother and be joined to his wife, and they shall become one flesh. And they were both naked, the man and his wife, and were not ashamed."* Soon as they obeyed Satan's instruction counter to

# -2-

# History of Conflict

what God gave, they became ashamed of something they were not ashamed of prior to receiving instructions other than from God.

My point is that the demonic realm led by Satan has one function, and one function only; to disseminate misinformation to mankind in general, and to Christians specifically, in order to alter the purpose of God. We need to recognize that, in altering the purpose of God, Satan attacked the throne of God first and led away a third of the angels.

His second point of attack was to attack God's human creation that was made in the image and likeness of God. Satan could not usurp God so he went after God's likeness and image in the form of Adam and Eve. The next natural progression of Satan's attack would be the children.

### *The Attack on Cain and Abel*

You are familiar with the story of Abel and Cain and their offering, Genesis 4:1-8. Let's start right where Satan makes his move. We will begin at the middle part of the last part of verse four in Genesis the fourth chapter. It says, *"And the Lord respected Abel and his offering, but He did not respect Cain and his offering. And Cain was very angry, and his countenance fell".* So the Lord said to Cain, asking him a question. *"Why are you angry? And why has your countenance fallen? If you do well, will you not be accepted?"* A lot of people don't understand

# -2-

# History of Conflict

what happened with Cain and God.

I will simply submit that the ground was cursed, (Gen. 3:17), because of what Adam and Eve did. Cain gave an offering from cursed ground, rather than a lamb's blood offering, like Abel did. So God rejected it and did not have respect for Cain's offering. As God explained to Cain in verse seven, *"If you do well will you not be accepted? And if you do not do well, sin lies at the door."*

Satan is the original sinner. He put sin into Adam and Eve and now he is transferring it into Cain's behavior. Now let's notice the second half of verse seven, and it states there; **"And its** (that is sin's) **desire is for you, but you should rule over it."** In other words, God told Cain, You should exercise will power (with the power of the true God), over your tendencies of anger because if you do not take control of it, it will take control of you.

> *Genesis 4:8 Now Cain talked with Abel his brother; and it came to pass, when they were in the field, that Cain rose up against Abel his brother and killed him.. (KJV)*

Obviously, Cain did not rule over the sin of anger or jealousy. He failed to rule over it and it led him to commit murder. We see the spiritual conflict being perpetrated on man by Satan when he attacked the throne of God and failed to de-throne God. Satan succeeded in confusing a third of the angels, confusing Adam and Eve, and leading Cain to murder. Satan has now confused and mislead The Church.

# -2-

# History of Conflict

This is some basic information to establish the fact biblically that spiritual warfare is a reality. It did not start in the New Testament, but it was pre Genesis1:2.

The war has been brought to the realm of human beings which includes we who are impacted by emotions, directives, inclinations, feelings, tendencies, urges, and impulses that are instigated by Satan and his kingdom. We have witnessed the impact that it had at the throne of God on our initial parents, Adam and Eve, and our initial siblings, Cain and Abel.

As we move forward we will review some scenarios where Satan manifested himself into the affairs of men and leaders of God to cause conflict, confusion, rebellion and sin among God's people. The Church is being continuously impacted today.

## **Future Event-Current Affairs**

Let's go to Revelations the twelfth chapter. I want to begin right there in verse seven. I want to encourage you again, to just move along with me using your Bible and making notes where you can or where you think it's applicable. Now moving to verse 7 in Revelations the twelfth chapter. It says here:

*Rev. 12:7And war broke out in heaven: Michael and his angels fought with the dragon; and the dragon and his angels fought, Rev 12:8 but they did not prevail, nor was a place found for them in heaven any longer. Rev*

# -2-

# History of Conflict

*12:9 So the great dragon was cast out, that serpent of old, called the Devil and Satan, who deceives the whole world; he was cast to the earth, and his angels were cast out with him. Rev12:10 Then I heard a loud voice saying in heaven, "Now salvation, and strength, and the kingdom of our God, and the power of His Christ have come, for the accuser of our brethren, who accused them before our God day and night, has been cast down. (NKJV)*

*Rev 12:11 "And they overcame him by the blood of the Lamb and by the word of their testimony, and they did not love their lives to the death. Rev 12:12 "Therefore rejoice, O heavens, and you who dwell in them! Woe to the inhabitants of the earth and the sea! For the devil has come down to you, having great wrath, because he knows that he has a short time." Rev 12:13 Now when the dragon saw that he had been cast to the earth, he persecuted the woman who gave birth to the male [Child]. Rev 12:14 But the woman was given two wings of a great eagle, that she might fly into the wilderness to her place, where she is nourished for a time and times and half a time, from the presence of the serpent.(NKJV)*

Now I wanted to share that particular pericope of scripture, because I wanted to reinforce the fact that we are engaged in a spiritual war. Spiritual war has a nature that's directed by an entity called Satan. Satan also attacks organizations, governments and situations.

# -2-

# History of Conflict

## *Satan Attacks Leaders*

An Episode with David, let's turn to I Chronicles 21:1. It says, ***"Now Satan stood up against Israel and moved David to number Israel"...*** In other words, Satan influenced David to number (take a census) Israel against the will of God. We know this is a problem because anytime Satan influences anybody, it is a problem. Let's look at verse seven in the same chapter of I Chronicles 21. It says there," ***And God was displeased with this thing; therefore He struck Israel. So David said to God, "I have sinned greatly, because I have done this thing"...*** David realized he was doing something God did not want him to do. Satan stood up against the nation of Israel and influenced the leadership (King David) to create a problem for the whole nation.

Satan does have impact and tries to interject himself into the plan of God to alter those who have been given direction. Another example of Satan having impact in the realm of man very directly is located in Job 1:6. It says, ***"Now there was a day when the sons of God came to present themselves before the Lord, and Satan also came among them."***

The angels are called the sons of God via creation not sons of God through adoption. Verse seven says, ***"And the Lord said to Satan, from where do you come?" So Satan answered the Lord and said, "From going to and fro on the earth, and from walking back and forth on it."*** Then the Lord said to Satan, ***"Have you considered my servant Job?"***

# -2-

# History of Conflict

We need to understand, God will sometimes point you out to Satan in order to see where you are in your Christian walk. It says:

> *Job 1:8-12" 1:8 Have you considered my servant Job that there is none like him on the earth, a blameless and upright man, one who fears God and shuns evil? 1:9 So Satan answered the Lord and said, "Does Job fear God for nothing? 1:10 Have You not made a hedge around him, around his household, and around all that he has on every side? You have blessed the work of his hands, and his possessions have increased in the land. 1:11 But now, stretch out Your hand and touch all that he has, and he will surely curse You to Your face! 1:12 And the Lord said to Satan "Behold, all that he has is in your power; only do not lay a hand on his person. So Satan went out from the presence of the Lord." (NKJV)*

When you read Job 1:13-22, you realize war broke out in the life of Job. My point is spiritual warfare is real and God wants to know where you stand. Satan has no power except for what God allows. He has no influence over you except what you give him. So what am I saying? Even though God allowed Satan to attack Job, Job still had the power to overcome what Satan said and did. Satan basically said, *"If you remove your protective hedge, Job will curse you to your face."*

Satan was counting on whatever he did to Job would force him into antichrist behavior. So we are looking at a level of warfare where Satan is trying to pull man off of his God given purpose. Satan has an agenda to pull men, women, children, and

# -2-

# History of Conflict

organizations including churches, off their main purpose, focus, mission and vision of God, the Father. God will always give us a clue through Jesus Christ, to what is happening in our lives, that is diverting us from his purpose.

### *A Word About Leviathan*

Let's move back to the book of Job, where in the middle of everything that Job is experiencing, there is chapter, forty one, that seems to be out of place, but it is not. It is exactly where it needs to be, because Job 41 does not talk about just a sea creature as some have interpreted. In Job 41:34, it says*: "He beholds every high thing; He is king over all the children of pride.* "The "He" referenced here, is Leviathan. It does not describe the level of power or influence of some giant fish in the ocean. Leviathan is a very powerful demon of pride. The reason God put chapter forty one, in this context, was and is to help us to understand that Job was having an issue with pride that was supernatural and not physical. If you go into chapter Job 42:1-2 it says, **"Then Job answered the Lord and said: I know that You can do everything, and that no purpose,"** In the King James it says **"that no thought can be withheld from You."**

Job was acknowledging; Lord, I know the issue was that You knew what I was thinking and although my behavior was righteous and all these other things were righteous, there was a sin of pride in me (Job), that You (God), wanted me to recognize and repent of. As we move on into the second half of Job 42:3, it says, **"...Therefore I have uttered what I did not understand,**

# -2-

# History of Conflict

**things too wonderful for me, which I did not know... I have heard of You by the hearing of the ear, But now my eye sees You."** Job's spiritual eyes were opened up. in verse six he says, **"Therefore I abhor myself, and repent in dust and ashes."**

So Job repented, once God allowed a trial to cause him to focus. Job did what Cain did not do. After much anguish he was able to stay with God's instructions and see what it was that he needed to change in his life. He took rule and charge over the sin, and did not allow it to rule over him. God restored him after he acknowledged his sin and repented of it.

The key to spiritual warfare is to acknowledge, recognize and repent of anything that is contrary to the Word of God. Before The Church can turn around from the confusion of compromise because of religious self-righteous pride, it has to do what Job did. The "Apostolic Manifesto Mandate", will be the voice of Godly reason.

### *Paganism Co-opted Christianity*

Early church leaders noted the pollution of the Christian faith with pagan ideologies as early as 230 A.D. It appears that Christians wanted to meet pagans halfway in order to bring them into the Christian faith. Combining abominable behavior and ungodly behavior with Christianity, does not make the behavior Christian or acceptable to Jesus Christ.

# -2-

# History of Conflict

*"This tendency on the part of Christians to meet Paganism half-way was very early developed; and we find Tertullian even in his day, about the year 230, bitterly lamenting the inconsistency of the disciples of Christ in this respect, and contrasting it with the strict fidelity of the pagans to their own superstition."(Hislop,1998, p.93)*

# Apostolic Manifesto

# -3-

# History of Counterfeit

Christian culture became saturated with pagan beliefs and religious practices. In the book of Revelation chapters two and three, Jesus Christ through John identifies all the problems He has with The Church. Jesus Christ is speaking to seven churches literally and, to all The Church figuratively and spiritually.

We only have to look at The Church today to see that the things Jesus Christ outlined through John in the book of Revelation are prevalent in The Church today. In fact, these things are running rampant in The Church. In many situations, The Church is proud of the degree of abominations and heresies that it supports.

> *Romans 1:24 Wherefore God also gave them up to uncleanness through the lusts of their own hearts, to dishonor their own bodies between themselves: Rom 1:27 And likewise also the men, leaving the natural use of the woman, burned in their lust one toward another; men with men working that which is unseemly, and receiving in themselves that recompence of their error which was meet. Rom 1:28And even as they did not like to retain God in [their] knowledge, God gave them over to a reprobate mind, to do those things which are not convenient; Rom 1:29 Being filled with all unrighteousness, fornication, wickedness, covetousness, maliciousness; full of envy, murder, debate, deceit, malignity; whisperers*

# -3-

# History of Counterfeit

*Rom1:30 Backbiters, haters of God, despiteful, proud, boasters, inventors of evil things, disobedient to parents, Rom 1:31 Without understanding, covenant breakers, without natural affection, implacable, unmerciful: Rom 1:32 Who knowing the judgment of God, that they which commit such things are worthy of death, not only do the same, but have pleasure in them that do them."(KJV)*

Not all churches and church leaders have conformed to heresy. Some have not conformed to this world, but to the Will of God, as it is states in Romans 12:1 –2:

> *"Romans 12:1-2 I beseech you therefore, brethren, by the mercies of God, that ye present your bodies a living sacrifice, holy, acceptable unto God, [which is] your reasonable service. Rom 12:2 And be not conformed to this world: but be ye transformed by the renewing of your mind, that ye may prove what [is] that good, and acceptable, and perfect, will of God."(KJV)*

Being religious and belonging to a religion or going to church is not necessarily being Godly. We must understand what legitimate Christianity is. We must understand the difference between Theology and Theocracy. We have too many theologians in The Church and not enough disciples that understand

# -3-

# History of Counterfeit

Theocracy. We need more theocrats in the body of Christ.

## *Origin of the Counterfeit*

Satan is the original counterfeiter (Isaiah 14 and Ezekiel 28), he wanted to be God and rule over God's creation, and still wants to. All he wants to do is create confusion, division, and controversy. This confusion exists today in churches around the world and in the hearts of people who believe because they belong to a church, they belong to Jesus Christ. Nothing could be further from the truth, and is the most devastating illusion of the Twenty-First Century Church.

## *Cain - Enoch*

The illusion started in the realm of man with Adam and Eve (Genesis 3), and was developed by Cain and his son Enoch (Genesis 4), and solidified by Constantine, the Roman Emperor. In the "Garden of Eden," Adam and Eve had a Theocracy, government directly from God, you could say government from God down. The tree of life represented government from God down. The tree of the knowledge of good and evil represented government from Satan down, Theology. A choice of Theocracy as opposed to Theology, Adam and Eve chose Theology.

# -3-

# History of Counterfeit

In the next section I want to focus on the evolution of Adam and Eve's wrong decision.

Cain and Abel represent the results of religious theological thinking. Cain represented a religious attitude as a result of Theology, and Abel represented a theocratic attitude as a result of Theocracy. Theological religion always murders, and attempts to murder, or co-opts God (Elohiym) Theocracy.

## How The Counterfeit Entered The Church

### *Enoch and Enoch*

I want to take a moment to address some pre-church history, relative to Satan's intent to produce a counterfeit of God's plan. There are two Enoch's listed in the Word of God. One is the son of Cain and the other was a son of Jared. In Genesis the fourth chapter you note the **Enoch,** the second from Adam son of Cain. In the fifth chapter of Genesis you note **Enoch,** the seventh from Adam. This is a very important distinction, because many believe that Genesis chapter five is a repeat of the fourth chapter of Genesis, that's simply not true.

Enoch, the son of Cain, descendants built structures, became skilled with musical instruments, and were artificers in brass and iron (Genesis 4: 20 – 22, KJV).

# -3-

# History of Counterfeit

Enoch, the son of Jared, was the one that "walked with God", (Genesis 5:24, KJV). When you read chapters four and five carefully you will see, that the line of Cain, the murderer, tried to rip off the anointing of the Godly descendants of Adam. Satan tried to replicate some of the names and did an exact with a few of the names to mislead. Because men lived for hundreds of years, the two Enoch's were contemporaries. Can you imagine the confusion of the people living during the time of the two Enoch's? My personal belief is that we are living in the same kind of parallel confusion today.

I suggest reading both chapters very carefully. Read the book of Jude that clearly distinguishes the seventh Enoch, the son of Jared, from Enoch the son of Cain. The **Counterfeit** and the false duplication, of the Word of God becomes institutionalized in the fourth chapter of Genesis. When one understands that Cain is not listed in the lineage of Adam, and the fact Cain chose Satan over the creator God, then one will realize that Cain chose Satanic religious behavior over true Godly Instructional Theocracy.

> *Gen 4:3 And in process of time it came to pass, that Cain brought of the fruit of the ground an offering unto the LORD. Gen 4:4 And Abel, he also brought of the firstlings of his flock and of the fat thereof. And the LORD had respect unto Abel and to his offering: Gen 4:5 But unto Cain*

26

# -3-

# History of Counterfeit

*and to his offering he had not respect. And Cain was very wroth, and his countenance fell. Gen 4:6 And the LORD said unto Cain, Why art thou wroth? And why is thy countenance fallen? Gen 4:7 If thou doest well, shalt thou not be accepted? and if thou doest not well, sin lieth at the door. And unto thee [shall be] his desire, and thou shalt rule over him. Gen 4:8 And Cain talked with Abel his brother: and it came to pass, when they were in the field, that Cain rose up against Abel his brother, and slew him. (KJV)*

We must beware of the way of Cain pointed out in Jude verse eleven; **"They have gone the way of Cain."** Cain brought an offering to God from ground that was still cursed, and murdered his brother. Cain's son Enoch started a religious structure based on a "cursed ground" mentality. Let's make sure that we don't fall into the same deception, and become promulgators of deception. Let's follow the example of the son of Jared, the Enoch that walked with God.

## *Emperor Constantine*

Constantine was the door opener to mixing pagan with Christ based practices. Many of our so called Christian celebrations come from this unholy

# -3-

# History of Counterfeit

union. We have become acclimated to accepting things without research.

*A major turning point in Christian history occurred when the Roman Emperor Constantine converted to Christianity. Whether this conversion was sincere or politically motivated, historians can only speculate. But the result was the end of persecution of Christians and the beginning of Christendom. In 313 Constantine issued the "Edict of Milan," which commanded official toleration of Christianity and other religions. He ordered that Sunday be granted the same legal rights as pagan feasts and that feasts in memory of Christian martyrs be recognized. Constantine outlawed the barbaric gladiatorial shows (although they persisted until the fifth century) and forbade Jews to stone to death other Jews who chose to become Christians. Contrary to popular belief, however, Constantine did not make Christianity the official religion of the empire. This was to be accomplished by Emperor Theodosius in 380. Constantine's program was one of toleration only, and he continued to support both Christianity and paganism. In 314, the cross appeared on Constantine's coins, but so did the figures of Sol Invictus and Mars Convervator. He raised his children as Christians and secured Christian clergy as personal advisors, but retained the title pontifex maximus, the chief*

# -3-

# History of Counterfeit

*priest of the state cult, until his death. (The Conversion of Constantine)*

The truth is what sets us free from bondage beliefs that have nothing to with the legitimate Theocratic Word of Jesus Christ.

*Jhn 4:23 But the hour cometh, and now is, when the true worshippers shall worship the Father in spirit and in truth: for the Father seeketh such to worship him. Jhn 4:24 God [is] a Spirit: and they that worship him must worship [him] in spirit and in truth...Jhn 8:32 And ye shall know the truth, and the truth shall make you free. (KJV)*

# Apostolic Manifesto

# -4-

# The Reformation

## *Mind Set*

The Reformation did a great deal to move The Church back toward a biblical foundation and open the Word of God to a wider range of people. The Word of God was no longer relegated to a few priests and higher ups in the Constantine model of The Church. Martin Luther, the father of the Reformation wanted The Church to move away from control by the elite back to the common man. He challenged the powers of The Church on several levels relative to who decides how Christians worship, what they believe and what they should and are ready to know about God.

The major areas of debate were and are who decides: doctrine, the priesthood, celibacy, holy orders, communion, church services, sacraments, marriage, veneration of saints, and salvation. Martin Luther challenged The Church, the "Catholic Church", relative to biblically based Christianity and what The Church was doing according to traditional Constantine Roman practices. Relative to doctrine, Luther argued that the Bible is the ultimate authority and that individuals have the right to make decisions based on what they read. He also believed in the priesthood of all believers, that each member had the right to act on the directives of the Holy Texts. Luther asserted that there was nothing in the Holy Texts that demanded or supported celibacy.

# -4-

# The Reformation

Relative to communion Luther believed that any Christian could perform mass or administer the sacraments, and that church services should be conducted in the language of the people and not exclusively in Latin. These are just a few of the arguments that Martin Luther put forth in an attempt to free Christianity from misinformed control. The Roman Catholic Church refused to accept Luther's arguments. As a result, Luther left The Church and the Lutheran or Protestant Reformation was born in 1517. The Reformation was supposed to produce a church that was closer to the Holy Scriptures and more accessible to the common man.

## *Denominations*

Some of the denominations that formed were: Lutheran, Methodist, Presbyterian, Covenant, Reformed, Moravian, Baptist, and United Church of Christ. Other movements such as Anabaptists, Pentecostal, Adventist, and the Holiness movement manifested as a result of the Reformation. During this period, there were many manifestations of transformation and renaissance relative to science, politics, and humanism. Other proponents such as John Calvin also emerged as a leader in Reform Theology.

# -4-

# The Reformation

### *God's Reformation*

God has always been a Theocrat and will always be a Theocrat. He is Alpha and Omega, the beginning and the end. He knows the beginning from the end. Jesus Christ is the Word and will be the Word. He was the Word from the beginning and God from the beginning. See the gospel of John chapter one. God the Father, God the Son, and the Holy Spirit; they are the Triune of Theocracy.

As we examine the history of God's contact with mankind according to the Word of God, the Holy Bible, it is apparent that God addressed mankind directly and from a perspective of Theocracy. Adam and Eve were Theocrats. They had direct contact with God, no mediator, no religious interpretation was necessary. The first religious interpreter was Satan himself, he began to interpret the Will of God and the Word of God for Eve. Then Eve shared her interpretation of the Word of God that she got from Satan, with Adam. Satan is the first "religious being", recorded in the Holy Texts, the Christian Bible.

Now from the point that Satan led Adam and Eve into rebellion, and religious thought, represented by the tree of the knowledge of good and evil, mankind has been studying Theology when he should have been practicing Theocracy. They were focusing on the tree of the knowledge of good and evil instead of

# -4-

# The Reformation

of the tree of life. For the last six thousand years there have been reformations away from and back to God. At this point in history God has issued an "Apostolic Manifesto Mandate", to return to Him. Jesus Christ came to Earth to reset and reboot the Plan of God, for all mankind. No efforts by Satan to dilute, confuse, delay, deny, or derail God's Reformation will prevail.

> *Matthew 16:18 And I say also unto thee, that thou art Peter, and upon this rock I will build my church; and the gates of hell shall not prevail against it. (KJV)*

We need to recognize that God is on the move, He's bringing about changes. He has set a "point of no return" order for us all.

> *Revelation 22:10 And he saith unto me, Seal not the sayings of the prophecy of this book: for the time is at hand. Rev 22:11 He that is unjust, let him be unjust still: and he which is filthy, let him be filthy still: and he that is righteous let him be righteous still: and he that is holy, let him be holy still. (KJV)*

## The Dark Ages

As we move to the next phase of this book, I want to address a significant topic. There is a period

# -4-

# The Reformation

of time in history called, the "Dark Ages", as far as The Church is concerned; a "truth black out" is how I would state it. Are we in a similar period now? I think it is important to make a statement relative to this period as it relates to the "Reformation" that occurred in The Church. It is important to note that this period is considered to have impacted the religious and secular arenas, primarily because of misinformation. I recommend reviewing this period (loosely considered to be from 400-1000 AD), for a more detailed statement and insight. A review, I believe, will assist in the understanding of the need for the "Reformation", and provide some insight into the next move of God.

# Apostolic Manifesto

# -5-

# Holy Spirit or Holy Ghost

I want to spend some time on a subject that is bound to create some controversy relative to the Holy Spirit. A lot of people in the Christian arena use the term Holy Ghost. In this season of God Shift, we must make sure that we are operating in the Holy Spirit and in the Truth of God. With all due respect, I take the God Shift Reformation approach to this issue.

## _A Little History_

First of all let me make it very clear, I believe in the Holy Spirit, that it is the third person of the Triune God regime and the power that sustains all legitimate Christianity. When I say legitimate Christianity, I'm talking about the Word of God, the Holy Scripture. I am not talking about traditions of men, nor denominations, or the bad habits that are passed down by folklore. I'm speaking of the Holy Logos and the Holy Rhēma Spirit of Elohiym.

I believe when we examine the Etymology, and the metaphysical and metaphorical uses of the terms spirit and ghost we will come to an interesting conclusion. After looking at many definitions of both words, and the fact that the word ghost derives from a German word Geist, not Hebrew nor Aramaic or Greek as in the Old and New Testaments respectively.

# -5-

# Holy Spirit or Holy Ghost

The Greek word (pneuma) that is derived from the Hebrew word (ruach) refer to the movement of air. Both the Hebrew and the Greek refer to the spirit. This trail leads to a word in Latin (spiritus), which has the benefit of being a precise translation, relative to the word spirit.

I think it would be important at this point to examine the behavior of a ghost spirit or the Holy Ghost, in relationship to the Holy Spirit of God. Ghosts have always been identified with haunting, terrorizing, demonization, and harassment. When we examine all the media programing about ghosts that are out there today; they are discussed as disembodied spirits wandering this earth looking for a place of rest.

Most of the movies, and literature that deal with paranormal activity, approach it from a perspective of evil ghost figures terrorizing, possessing, and using human beings to, destroy one another like zombies. I find it hard to believe that a society of people, who have been conditioned through the media, and reality, to perceive a ghost to be holy, Holy as it relates to God. This is not just an issue of so called harmless semantics, but an issue of perception and reality.

# -5-

# Holy Spirit or Holy Ghost

Now in contrast what does the Holy Spirit do? Well, the Word of God can provide some insight relative to that. The Holy Spirit has a resume that speaks for Himself. Now let's see what the Holy Spirit of God has to say, about Himself; as articulated by Jesus Christ directly, and through the pen of the gospel writers' testimony of power.

## *Support Scriptures*

I want to start in the sixteenth chapter of the Gospel of John. Christ Himself outlines the character of the Holy Spirit.

> *Jhn 16:7 "Nevertheless I tell you the truth. It is to your advantage that I go away; for if I do not go away, the Helper will not come to you; but if I depart, I will send Him to you. Jhn 16:8 "And when He has come, He will convict the world of sin, and of righteousness, and of judgment: Jhn 16:9 "of sin, because they do not believe in Me; Jhn 16:10 "of righteousness, because I go to My Father and you see Me no more; Jhn 16:11 "of judgment, because the ruler of this world is judged. (NKJV)*

The Holy Spirit has very specific assignments, and not one of them involves haunting houses, running around and rattling chains, behaving like a poltergeist and operating in false gifts.

# -5-

# Holy Spirit or Holy Ghost

Let me make a point here about what people believe relative to a ghost spirit. They believe that a ghost spirit is the spirit of a dead human being, roaming the earth trying to find peace, resolution, or to get even.

There is nothing holy about any of those activities. All one has to do is to look at history, the occult, and what's being produced by movie companies and television stations. Really, how can we truly attach the term holy to the term ghost, after understanding the terms, historical origins, functions, and what they stand for? A dictionary would easily clear this up. The term Holy Ghost is an oxy-moron; one could say a paradox.

> *"A noun, figure of speech in which apparently contradictory terms appear in conjunction (e.g., faith unfaithful kept him falsely true)."Oxymorons. Rhetoric, a figure of speech by which a locution produces an incongruous, seemingly self-contradictory effect, as in "cruel kindness" or "to make haste slowly." Origin:1650–60; Late Latin Oxymoron presumed Greek, oxymoron neuter of Oxymoros. (Dictionary.com)*

> *"Paradox a similar figure of speech to paradox is oxymoron. Below are examples of paradox: Smart dummy (you cannot be smart and dumb at the same time)."(Reference.com)*

# -5-

# Holy Spirit or Holy Ghost

*"Antonym, a noun a word opposite in meaning to another. Fast is an antonym of slow. Compare Synonym, a noun a word having the same or nearly the same meaning as another in the language, as happy, joyful, elated." (Dictionary.com)*

To the contrary, the "Holy Spirit" is not an oxymoron but is an antonym to the term "Holy Ghost." The Holy Spirit would be a synonym, to terms like righteous one, spirit of peace, spirit of joy, and the spirit power. God the Father of all creation is Holy, Righteous and Powerful. I think the point has been made. Let's look again at the Word of God, for validation.

*Jhn 14:26 "But the Helper, the Holy Spirit, whom the Father will send in My name, He will teach you all things, and bring to your remembrance all things that I said to you. Jhn 20:22 And when He had said this, He breathed on [them], and said to them, "Receive the Holy Spirit." Act1:2 until the day in which He was taken up, after He through the Holy Spirit had given commandments to the apostles whom He had chosen. (NKJV)*

*Act 1:5 for John truly baptized with water, but you shall be baptized with the Holy Spirit not many days from now. Act 1:8 "But you shall receive power when the Holy Spirit has come upon you; and you shall be witnesses to Me in Jerusalem, and in all Judea and Samaria, and to the end of the earth. (NKJV)*

# -5-

# Holy Spirit or Holy Ghost

I am going to close this section by simply stating it is not my intention to falsely judge, or accuse anyone who uses the term "Holy Ghost." But I have to point out what the Word of God says about the matter. Jesus Christ is not dead, He sits at that the right hand of God the Father, working through the Holy Spirit. The Holy Spirit is not a wandering spirit of angry dead people. Ghosts are disembodied spirits that have nothing to do with "Holiness." I recommend that you do your own research and come to your own conclusion.

> *Mat 22:32 'I am the God of Abraham, the God of Isaac, and the God of Jacob'? God is not the God of the dead, but of the living." Mar 12:27 "He is not the God of the dead, but the God of the living. You are therefore greatly mistaken." Luk 20:38 "For He is not the God of the dead but of the living, for all live to Him."(NJKV)*

Let me just say that there's nothing new about this subject, or the debate that surrounds it. We need to be careful that we don't get caught up in doctrinal theological tradition. We don't want to be caught up in Theological behavior, and ignore the reality and the truth of Theocracy.

# -5-

# Holy Spirit or Holy Ghost

*Holy Ghost is the correct term doctrinally. Although the original meaning of ghost is spirit, the King James translators were not ignorant of the modern connotations... The word carried the meaning of a "disembodied spirit of a dead person appearing among the living" by the fourteenth century. It would have been well-known to the King James translators as having this meaning. Therefore, since they also used Holy Spirit (Luke 11:13) and could have easily used that term exclusively, there must have been a distinct reason for retaining Holy Ghost. Certainly, one of the reasons is that it was an established theological term. (Why The holy Ghost)*

You have to wonder why if the term "Holy Ghost", was in question why use it? Why risk using a term that may conjure up something opposite to the intent of God?

*Here is the problem. The KJV is the only version that uses the terminology Holy Ghost." Unbeknownst to many KJV "only" folks the words "Holy Ghost" are not found even one time in the Old Testament in the King James Version. What words ARE found there? Holy Spirit. The phrase - (Holy Spirit) is found three times in the Old Testament (KJV and interestingly enough ...the phrase - Holy Spirit - is even used FOUR times in the KJV New Testament!*

# -5-

# Holy Spirit or Holy Ghost

*In both the Old and New Testaments the KJV sometimes capitalizes spirit and/or holy and sometimes not. In Psalm 51:11, (KJV) David prays "Take not thy holy spirit from me." The Old Testament word for spirit is RUACH- the KJV translators translate it correctly as "spirit." Never do they translate RUACH as "ghost." The Hebrew word for "expire" or "to die" is often translated in the KJV in the Old English manner of saying "he gave up the ghost." Again, not the correct Hebrew expression or even the modern English expression. (Why The King James Version)*

Again, some may say why make a big issue about this it's just a matter of semantics. In the spiritual realm things are very precise and technical relative to power and authority. God will look on the heart, but it is up to us to make sure we are operating at a Godly level of accuracy. Because a proper understanding and/or a misunderstanding, will and has changed the outcome of human history. Let's review one famous example of word placement and usage, relative to Satanic manipulation. I have referred to this scenario previously, but it is worth restating to make the case of semantics.

*Gen 2:15 And the LORD God took the man, and put him into the garden of Eden to dress it and to keep it. Gen 2:16 And the LORD God commanded the man, saying, Of every tree of the garden thou mayest freely eat: Gen 2:17*

# -5-

# Holy Spirit or Holy Ghost

*But of the tree of the knowledge of good and evil, thou shalt not eat of it: for in the day that thou eatest thereof thou shalt surely die. (KJV)*

Now let's observe the game of semantics, used by Satan to change the course of human history. God simply told Adam if he ate from the tree of the Knowledge of Good and Evil that he would die. Satan came alone and said the opposite, by just adding the word "not," into the statement" thou shalt **not** surely die.

> *Gen 3:1 Now the serpent was more subtil than any beast of the field which the LORD God had made. And he said unto the woman, Yea, hath God said, Ye shall not eat of every tree of the garden? (KJV)*
>
> *Gen 3:2 And the woman said unto the serpent, we may eat of the fruit of the trees of the garden: Gen 3:3 But of the fruit of the tree which [is] in the midst of the garden, God hath said, Ye shall not eat of it, neither shall ye touch it, lest ye die. Gen 3:4 And the serpent said unto the woman, Ye shall not surely die. (KJV)*

Yes, I have made reference to this particular pericope of text earlier in this book. But the point I'm making at this time is that how we use terms, and words does matter. As servants of the one and only true "Triune God" regime, we need to get it correct. Satan is very clever and we need to be aware, that he

# -5-

# Holy Spirit or Holy Ghost

will use every loophole to deceive us. I am redundant with a purpose.

## *End Note*

Adam and Eve did die within that one thousand year day period of God.  In fact no human being has lived the prophetic one thousand year day. It will happen in the Millennium.

**Gen2:16 And the LORD God commanded the man, saying, of every tree of the garden thou mayest freely eat: Gen 2:17 But of the tree of the knowledge of good and evil, thou shalt not eat of it: for in the day that thou eatest thereof thou shalt surely die.**

**2Pe 3:8 But, beloved, be not ignorant of this one thing, that one day [is] with the Lord as a thousand years, and a thousand years as one day. (KJV)**

**Rev 20:6 Blessed and holy [is] he that hath part in the first resurrection: on such the second death hath no power, but they shall be priests of God and of Christ, and shall reign with him a thousand years. (KJV)**

# -5-

# Holy Spirit or Holy Ghost

The Holy Triune God is paying attention, we should pay attention; He will carry out His Word.

> *Lam 2:17 The LORD has done what He purposed; He has fulfilled His word Which He commanded in days of old. (NKJV)*

# Apostolic Manifesto

# -6-

# Supernatural Implications

We've only scratched the surface relative to the impact of the period we call the Reformation. But we do want to move forward and try to understand the supernatural implications. We want to examine some World View's relative to that, in order to understand what The Church has been up against, and still is up against relative to Satanic attack. We have established Satan's intrusion into the Theocracy of God relative to His will for man. We need to review the reality of the attack on mankind individually and corporately. Organizations are under attack as well as individuals. And we need to understand that there is a real supernatural attempt to destroy God's Will in the natural.

## *Principalities and Powers*

The principalities and powers text is often discussed in context with the putting on the armor of God in Ephesians 6:13.

> *For we wrestle not against flesh and blood, but against principalities, against powers, against the rulers of the darkness of this world, against spiritual wickedness in* high places. *(Ephesians 6:12, KJV).*

Francis Frangipone asserts that the heavenly places is a battleground arena where we should be prepared to do battle.

49

# -6-

# Supernatural Implications

> *Thus, our purpose here is to help equip you for battle in each of the three primary battlegrounds: the mind, the church and the heavenly places. (Frangipane, 1989, p.7)*

John Eckhardt reinforces the same mind set in Peter Wagner's book, *New Apostolic Churches*, as part of the apostolic anointing. He also contends that the principalities and powers must be challenged.

> *The first thing the Lord gave the Twelve when He sent them out was power against unclean spirits' (Matt.10:1(KJV). The apostolic anointing is therefore recognized in the spirit realm. A level of power an authority that is released through apostles and apostolic churches must be acknowledged by the demonic and angelic realm... The principalities and powers that have gripped multitudes of people for so long must be challenged by implementing this kind of power and authority. (Wagner, 1998, p. 50)*

Frangiopane and Eckhardt imply more than just a deliverance ministry for individuals who may be demonically afflicted, but suggest a ministry for warriors battling the entire spirit realm. Whenever they attempt to influence, manipulate, and control, whenever they choose to manifest.

Walter Wink comments on the powers from the perspective of manifestations. Wink implies that the powers operate through churches, nations, and economies from the invisible realm.

# -6-

# Supernatural Implications

*Every Power tends to have a visible pole, and outer form be it a church, a nation, or an economy and an invisible pole, an inner spirit or driving force that animates, legitimates, and regulates its physical manifestation in the world. (Wink, 1984, p.5)*

In my opinion, Bill Wylie-Kellerman makes an important statement regarding the principalities and powers in their manifested forms, and the failure of moral theology in the American context to confront them.

*What is most crucial about this situation, biblically speaking, is the failure of moral theology, in the American context, to confront the principalities, the institutions, systems, ideologies, and other political and social powers as militant, aggressive, and immensely influential creatures in this world as it is. (Wylie-Kellerman, 1991, p. 71)*

Relative to principalities and powers, I agree with the authors and believe that this is a major battleground in the deliverance ministry/spiritual warfare arena. I believe prayer is the major weapon in engaging the principalities and powers in all of their invisible and physical manifestations. As far as Christians are concerned, The Church is one forum where the principalities and powers should be confronted and ultimately defeated.

# -6-

# Supernatural Implications

## World View(s)

World view in the context of religion focuses on the spiritual and the material; some may state it as the supernatural and natural. The World has a perception relative to an overall belief about what controls or influence existence, what is considered real or realistic or what is not. I have selected several authors' perspectives, Dr. L. David Mitchell's, Dr. Ed Murphy's and Walter Wink's relative to World View.

### Dr. L. David Mitchell

*By 'world view' we mean that mental framework which gives shape to our existence. Our world view integrates our knowledge and understanding of this world, our perceptions about human life, about moral social realities, and about our reason for existence. For Christians, as for humankind naturally the realm of spiritually good and evil is part of their world view. (Mitchell, 1999, p.31)*

*God and the realm of angels, with Satan and his demons, provide the spiritual background, the framework against which men and women and children live out their lives. Their lives are, in turn, not only physical lives in a material world, but spiritual ones. In every human heart there is a 'nostalgia' for heaven and a reality that is far greater than all we presently see. Every human being has a sense of the numinous, of the transcendent and righteous Creator. For the practitioner of 'primal religion', the animist, every occurrence is fraught with spiritual meaning. The*

# -6-

# Supernatural Implications

*universe is open with a blurred line between natural and supernatural. The material world integrates with the realm of gods and spirits. (Mitchell, 1999, p. 30)*

Mitchell discusses physical lives in a material world being spiritual lives as well. He proposes that the universe is open, having a blurred line between natural and supernatural, integrating with dimension of gods and spirits.

## Dr. Ed Murphy

Aside from the agnostic position, only two conceivable world views exist according to Murphy. The spiritualistic world view and materialistic or naturalistic world view.

*The spiritualistic world view affirms that ultimate reality is spiritual: immaterial, not physical or material. According to this view; whether ultimate reality is looked upon as personal or impersonal, it is spiritual. The vast majority of the world's more than five billion inhabitants hold to some form of a spiritualistic world view. Intellectually convinced atheists are very rare even in Western and in Marxist societies. Ours is not a world of philosophical materialists, but of convinced spiritualists. (Murphy, 1996, p. 3)*

*Second, the materialistic or naturalistic world view affirms that ultimate reality is material or physical, not spiritual. This view assumes that all life generated spontaneously from nonlife and that by this process*

# -6-

# Supernatural Implications

*primitive single-celled life forms evolved over vast periods of time in to the vast range of life as we know it today. (Murphy, 1996, p. 4)*

Murphy setting aside the agnostic perspective dialogues on the spiritual and materialistic world views. He asserts that the vast majority of the World's population, about five billion hold to some kind of variation of the spiritual world view concept as he has outlined it to be. I could subscribe to the spiritualistic world view as articulated by Murphy.

## Walter Wink

Wink identifies five world view perspectives that deserve some review.

> *The Ancient Worldview [sic]. This is the worldview reflected in the Bible. In this conception everything earthly has its heavenly counterpart, and everything heavenly has its earthly counterpart. Every event is thus a simultaneity of both dimensions of reality. (Wink, 1992, p. 4)*

This world view concept is in my opinion is simplistic and consistent with my Theocracy.

> *The Spiritualistic Worldview. What distinguishes this world view from all other types is that it divides human beings into 'soul' and 'body'; one understands oneself as the same as one's 'soul' and other than one's'*

# -6-

# Supernatural Implications

*body.' In this account, the created order is evil, false, corrupted. Creation was itself the fall. Matter is either indifferent or downright evil. Earthly life is presided over by imperfect and evil Powers. (Wink, 1992, p. 4)*

I have some problems with the Spiritualistic world view concept, relative to Creation being the fall. Also, the statement relative to the evil and corrupted nature of the created order, presents a problem relative to the Theocratic paradigm I subscribe to.

*The Materialistic world view....In Many ways the antithesis of the world-rejection of spiritualism. In this view, there is no heaven, no spiritual world, no God, no soul nothing but material existence and what can be known through the five senses and reason. The spiritual world is an illusion. (Wink, 1992, p. 5)*

The Materialistic World View became prominent in the Enlightenment age, and in my opinion is anti- God. The Materialistic world view perspective is the opposite of everything I would adhere to as a Christian and Theocrat no heaven, no spiritual world, no soul, or God; only an existence of the five senses and reason.

*The" Theological" Worldview. In reaction to materialism, Christian theologians invented the supernatural... Acknowledging that this supersensible realm could not be known by the senses, they conceded earthly reality to modern science and preserved a privileged 'spiritual' realm immune to confirmation or refutation at the cost of an integral view of reality and the simultaneity of heavenly and earthly aspects of existence. (Wink, 1992, p. 5)*

# -6-

# Supernatural Implications

This world view concept is not consistent with what I embrace. The idea that Christian invented supernaturalism, precludes the ideology that God is the supernatural being who created the natural as well as the supernatural realm.

> *The Integral Worldview. This new word view... is emerging from a confluence of sources: the reflections of Carl Jung, Telhard de Chardin, Morton Kelsey, Thomas Berry, Matthew Fox, process philosophy, and the new physics. It sees everything as having an outer and an inner aspect. It attempts to take seriously the spiritual insights of the ancient or biblical worldview by affirming a withinness or interiority in all things, but sees this inner spiritual reality as inextricably related to an outer concretion or physical manifestation. It is no more intrinsically 'Christian' than the ancient worldview, but I believe it makes the bible data more intelligible for people today than any other available worldview, including the ancient (Wink, 1992, p. 5)*

This world view is also one that reflects dimensions of my Theocracy and Christianity. I could embrace this world view cautiously.

From my perspective, time spent with the world view concept relative to Christianity is important to this treatise. The issue of spiritual warfare, exorcism, and demonization is impacted by the world view that focuses on spiritual and the material, or the natural and the supernatural. It is important to understand what the thinking is, from a global perspective.

# -6-

# Supernatural Implications

I subscribe to the Spiritualistic World View, proposed by Murphy. Note how the Spiritualistic World View proposed by Murphy differs from the one proposed by Wink. I would also state that Mitchell describes a mindset that I could embrace without conflict. The Ancient World View and the Integral World View would also fit into Theocracy. These four world view positions that I have selected to embrace best describe how I operate relative to the Apostolic Manifesto.

Some information for this chapter was extracted from my book, *"Impact of A Deliverance Prayer", A Study of Deliverance Ministry.* This book is an **Apologetics** on "Inner Healing and Deliverance."

*Apologetics 1. The branch of theology concerned with the defense and rational justification of Christianity 2. A defensive method of argument. (dictionary.com)*

For more information on the subjects of demons and deliverance I recommend my book. *www.dremaddox.org*

# Apostolic Manifesto

# -7-

# Problem Clarification

## Cold Hard Facts

The first thing we have to do is to acknowledge that there is a problem, and stop hiding our heads in the sand. The fact of the matter is that there is as much adultery, fornication, divorce, homosexuality, lying, stealing, pedophile behavior, drunkenness and drug use; among believers as it is among so-called nonbelievers. Crimes are being committed in church by leaders and members of The Church during church services. They go undetected and or unreported; review the stats for yourself.

We've gotten to the point where we want to cover things up to protect reputations and people who make large donations to The Church. We use terms like, mercy, love, patience, understanding, and forgiveness, to cover up crimes committed against children, women, and the powerless.

*The church consists of people called out from the pagan world. With the second phrase, church of the living God, Paul reminds the readers how God has called them out from a pagan world. This "assembly" of Christian people is distinct from the other assemblies of the world because the living God dwells within it (2 Cor 6:16). The privilege of being called out to live in God's presence carries with it, however, the responsibility to live a life worthy of the One who has called. God's calling of the Hebrews out of Egypt into association with himself required them to be holy (Lev 11:45); and membership in the church of the living*

# -7-

# Problem Clarification

*God makes the same demand; compare 1Pet 1:15-16.*
*(The Motivation and Mystery of Godly Behavior)*

The Great God, the Father of Lights calls mankind out of a pagan society. To bring them into freedom and the mechanism to accomplish what is supposed to be The Church. The Church is composed of people with problems, but they are not supposed to grow greater in the skills of Satan and sin. The Church is supposed to be a place where you learn to divorce yourself of sin. Church should not be a place where you learn to put on a tuxedo, dress sin up, look good, righteous, and religious, but not change a thing in your life.

*The church exists to protect and promote the truth. Paul employs building imagery in the last descriptive phrase to characterize the church in terms of one of its major functions: the pillar and foundation of the truth. As the "supporting foundation" (one idea is expressed rather than two) of the truth, the believing church is the guardian and communicator of the gospel in the world. This aspect of the church also demands from believers appropriate conduct: godly leadership, that the message might not be discredited, and corporate prayer for the missionary enterprise, that the message might be spread. (The Motivation and Mystery of Godly Behavior)*

Romans the twelfth chapter versus one and two, also point out the fact that we cannot be conformed to this world.

# -7-

# Problem Clarification

But The Church today rather than reforming the world and society, has allowed the world and society to reform it. The Church has sanctioned what God called abominations, we celebrate what God won't tolerate, we hold high what God has laid low; and we take pleasure in it.

I would highly recommend a prayerful, meditative reading of Romans the first chapter. Actually I strongly encourage that you should actually be fasting when you read Romans the first chapter, it is a powerful indictment of mankind, because they refused the truth of God. That indictment stands on The Church today because of the same refusal to embrace the truth.

A great part of The Church has been turned over to a reprobate mind. We no longer seek the Holiness of God, but wholeness with men. The Church needs to wake up, and represent the shed blood of Jesus Christ. God does not adjust His Word or His Will based on the current political correctness.

*Rom1:28 And even as they did not like to retain God in [their] knowledge, God gave them over to a reprobate mind, to do those things which are not convenient; Rom 1:29 Being filled with all un-righteousness, fornication, wickedness, covetousness, maliciousness; full of envy ,deceit, malignity; whisperers, Rom 1:30 Backbiters, haters of God, despiteful, proud, boasters, inventors of evil things, disobedient to parents, Rom 1:31 Without understanding, covenant breakers, without natural affection, implacable, unmerciful: (KJV)*

# -7-

# Problem Clarification

*Rom 1:32 Who knowing the judgment of God, that they which commit such things are worthy of death, not only do the same, but have pleasure in them that do them. (KJV)*

We have become Theological thinker's more than Theocratic practitioners. We want to interpret the Word of God, rather than submit to the Word of God. We indeed have become Religious thinkers and Babylonian citizens.

## The Demonic Traps

The Church has fallen into several traps as we discussed earlier relative to what took place in the Garden of Eden, Genesis the third chapter. Satan has three basic attack techniques; the lust of the flesh, lust of the eyes, and the pride of life. It worked on Adam and Eve, the nation of Israel, and has worked and is now working on and in The Church.

> *1Joh 2:15 Love not the world, neither the things [that are] in the world. If any man love the world, the love of the Father is not in him. 1 Joh 2:16 For all that [is] in the world, the lust of the flesh, and the lust of the eyes, and the pride of life, is not of the Father, but is of the world. (KJV)*

# -7-

# Problem Clarification

Instead of us who claim to be church people and Christians shining a light into the world, we have allowed the world to shine darkness into The Church. We work at adjusting our eyes to the darkness rather than stepping into the light, see John chapter three.

> *Jhn3:19 And this is the condemnation, that light is come into the world, and men loved darkness rather than light, because their deeds were evil. Jhn3:20 For everyone that doeth evil hateth the light, neither cometh to the light, lest his deeds should be reproved. Jhn3:21But he that doeth truth cometh to the light, that his deeds may be made manifest, that they are wrought in God. (KJV)*

### *Lust of the Flesh-Antichrist Spirit*

Now we want to talk about the diabolical spirit of antichrist. The **Spirit of Antichrist** will cause one to deny the existence, deity, and teachings of Jesus Christ. One could deny the fact that He was human as well as God. One could deceive and manipulate His Word, and operate in lawlessness, which is totally separate from who, what, and where Christ is. The tendency is to do things based on how we feel, how we think, and what we know. We want to operate out of our flesh, rather than let Christ operate through our flesh. Let's turn to first John the forth chapter, and it just simply says here,

# -7-

# Problem Clarification

*1Joh.4:3 And every spirit that confesseth not that Jesus Christ is come in the flesh is not of God: and this is that [spirit] of antichrist, whereof ye have heard that it should come; and even now already is in the world. (KJV)*

This attitude is one that denies Christ. Now many people say, "Well, if I ask someone, did Christ come in the flesh?" and they say "Yes," then they are okay. That's just part of the question. The other part is, "He's coming in the flesh now." In John the fourteenth chapter, let's go there, because I want to make this point very clear. Because if you don't understand this, you can ask that question, and still be deceived. *Jesus answered and said to them,*

*Joh. 14:23 Jesus answered and said unto them, If anyone loves Me, he will keep My word; and My Father will love him, and We will come to him and make Our home with him. (NKJV)*

Some translations say "abode," but it simply means, that the Father and Christ will be in you, and we know that in John 16 He is going to also send the Holy Spirit. So they are all going to be abiding in you. So when we read that statement in first John, what it is really saying is that you need to verify whether or not a person can confess that Jesus Christ literally came in the flesh and lived, and was flesh and spirit, human and God; and is living in the flesh of legitimate Saints today.

# -7-

# Problem Clarification

He also is constantly reproducing His mentality in us. Because we're supposed to have the mind of Christ, and the mind of Christ is the same as the mind of the Father. So if we have Him, we have the Father, the Son and the Holy Spirit abiding in us now; an antichrist mentality will never confess that. What is The Church confessing?

## *Lust of The Eyes-Rebellion Witchcraft*

Let's move to first Samuel. If you read the whole chapter you'll see that Saul did several things that he wasn't told to do, and tried to justify them before God. Samuel finally told him in verse twenty three.

> *1 Sam.15:23 For rebellion is as the sin of witchcraft, And stubbornness is as iniquity and idolatry. Because you have rejected the word of the LORD, He also has rejected you from being king. (NKJV)*

Saul acted based on what he saw, based on the reaction of people. So the point is, that a rejection of God's instruction led to a rejection of King Saul's kingship, over the nation of Israel. In the Garden of Eden what Adam and Eve saw in the tree of the "Knowledge of Good and Evil" led them to rebellion, and being ejected from the Garden of Eden.

# -7-

# Problem Clarification

I just want to make an interesting point here. Some of you who will be reading this have children who are of age who don't want to obey God but want to live in your house. God, the "Original Parent", when Adam and Eve disobeyed the rules of the house, He put them out. He did not only put them out; He put an angel and a flaming sword to keep them from getting back in. That did not mean He did not care for them.

He provided them with clothes and He was concerned for them. But they could not stay in His house, the Garden of Eden, in a state of rebellion. We need to understand that a state of rebellion is paramount to witchcraft, witchcraft is paramount to demonization or demon activity. This is a point of attack.

If Satan can get you off point with the Word of God, then he can lure you into a level of confusion.

> *Galatians 1:8-9 But though we, or an angel from heaven, preach any other gospel unto you than that which we have preached unto you, let him be accursed. Gal 1:9 As we said before, so say I now again, If any [man] preach any other gospel unto you than that ye have received, let him be accursed. (KJV)*

# -7-

# Problem Clarification

Church leadership cannot allow what it sees as politics, political correctness, social science, psychology, or any other influence to lead them away from instruction received from Jesus Christ. We can't make decisions based on what we perceive with our eyes, we will be tempted to go against Godly instructions, because what we may see may be contrary to and in conflict with the Will of God.

The Church has found a comfort zone, based on observational decision making. We need to walk by faith and not by sight. *"For we walk by faith, not by sight,"* **(2 Corinthians 5:7 KJV)**. We need to stay focused on the Word of God and concentrate on keeping our eyes on Him. His instructions should be followed implicitly.

## *Pride of Life - King Leviathan*

*"He beholds every high thing; He is king over all the children of pride".* *(Job 41:34 NKJV)* That does not describe the level of power or influence of some giant fish in the ocean. He, Leviathan was pointed out to help us to understand that Job was having an issue with pride that was supernatural and not physical. When you go into chapter forty two it says, *"Then Job answered the LORD and said: "I know that You can do everything, and that no purpose of yours can be withheld from you"* (Job 42:1-2 NKJV).

67

# -7-

# Problem Clarification

In the King James it says that no **"thought *can be withheld from You."*** Job was acknowledging; Lord, I knew the issue was that You knew what I was thinking. Although Job's behavior was thought to be righteous and religious, he knew his thoughts were not righteous. There was a sin of pride in Job that God wanted him to recognize, and repent of that sin. As we move on in the second half of verse three in chapter forty two it says, ***"Therefore I have uttered what I did not understand, Things too wonderful for me, which I did not know."*** (Job 42:3 NKJV)

Then he goes on to say, ***"I have heard of You by the hearing of the ear, But now my eye sees You."*** Job's spiritual eyes were opened up, (verse 5). In verse six he says, ***"Therefore I abhor myself, And repent in dust and ashes",*** (verse 6). So Job repented; once God allowed a catastrophic trial to cause him to focus. Job did what Cain did not do, he repented.

After much anguish he was able to stay with God's instructions and see what it was that he needed to change in his life and he took ruler ship and charge over it. He did not allow it to rule over him, and God restored him after he acknowledged his sin and repented of it. So that is the key, to be able to do in spiritual warfare what Job did at the end. That was to acknowledge, recognize and repent of anything that's contrary to the Word of God. Is The Church too full of pride to repent and return to God?

# -7-

# Problem Clarification

## *Summary*

Jesus Christ made it very clear that we are supposed to season the society as salt and brighten the world with our light. Instead The Church has been flavored by the world and we choose to hide our light. Could you truly say that Christ's would applaud The Church today? Would He say the majority of The Church was on target?

> *Mat 5:13 Ye are the salt of the earth: but if the salt have lost his savour, wherewith shall it be salted? It is thenceforth good for nothing, but to be cast out, and to be trodden under foot of men. Mat 5:14 Ye are the light of the world. A city that is set on an hill cannot be hid.*

> *Mat 5:15 Neither do men light a candle, and put it under a bushel, but on a candlestick; and it giveth light unto all that are in the house. Mat 5:16 Let your light so shine before men, that they may see your good works, and glorify your Father which is in heaven. (KJV)*

When someone speaks against what is happening in The Church (sin), they are labeled and rebuked with statements like we shouldn't judge, or God has given us Grace to do what we're doing, "to sin and not truly repent." The Word of God says we will judge the world and angels and Grace is not a license to sin. Read first Corinthians the sixth chapter, and Romans the sixth chapter.

# -7-

# Problem Clarification

The Word of God will reveal something different from the tradition of men. Let the Word of God be true, and not the hearsay and heresy of men.

> *1Cr 6:2 Do ye not know that the saints shall judge the world? And if the world shall be judged by you, are ye unworthy to judge the smallest matters? 1Cr 6:3 Know ye not that we shall judge angels? how much more things that pertain to this life?. Rom 6:1 What shall we say then? Shall we continue in sin, that grace may abound? Rom 6:2 God forbid. How shall we, that are dead to sin, live any longer therein? (KJV)*

One of the main mandates of the "Apostolic Manifesto" is to bring alignment in reference to the Word of God. We must lift up our voices and identify the vicious, venomous, insidious, cancerous and toxicity of sin toleration in The Church also known as the Body of Jesus Christ. We must lift up our voices and proclaim, orate, declare, preach and teach the Word of God. We must set the example, we, meaning you and I.

We must articulate as well as demonstrate, righteousness, holiness and godly purity. We have to lift up our voices in defense of the Holy Gospel.

> *Isa 58:1 Cry aloud, spare not, lift up thy voice like a trumpet, and shew my people their transgression, and the house of Jacob their sins. (KJV)*

# Apostolic Manifesto

# -8-

# The Apostolic Manifesto

## Definitions

### *Manifesto*

I would define "Manifesto" as a written statement that describes the policies, goals, and opinions of a person or group. A public declaration of intentions, opinions, objectives, or motives, as one issued by a government, sovereign, or organization. A simple non-complicated definition of Manifesto; that it is basically a written declarative of a position, or positions, from a particular point of origin. This is an extrapolated definition from several sources.

Some areas of origin have been stated above. Now, how does this definition fit into the context of Apostolic Manifesto?

### *Apostolic Manifesto*

Considering the basic definition(s) of the word manifesto, we can construct a working definition of and for **Apostolic Manifesto**. A written statement that describes the policies, goals, and opinions of the one Creator God. A public declaration of intentions, opinions, objectives, or motives, as issued by the one true God of the universe. A written declarative of a position, or positions, from a Theocratic point of origin and or world view.

# -8-

# The Apostolic Manifesto

## *The Who*

Based on the above definition, the written mandate is the Holy Bible. The Father, Son, and the Holy Spirit are the authors. The Apostolic Manifesto is for all creation, and The Church is the vehicle of delivery. The Apostles, Prophets, Evangelists, Pastors and Teachers; have the responsibility of articulating the Manifesto of *Elohiym,* the mighty Triune God.

Jesus Christ is the spokesman (Word) of the mighty Triune. In John chapter one verse one; *"In the beginning was the Word, and the Word was with God, and the Word was God."* Also see verse two. *(KJV)*

Ephesians the fourth chapter beginning in verse nine through thirteen. This pericope of Scripture, lays out the structure of the Apostolic Manifesto delivery system.

> *Eph 4:9 Now that he ascended, what is it but that he also descended first into the lower parts of the earth? Eph4:10 He that descended is the same also that ascended up far Above all heavens, that he might fill all things. Eph 4:11 And he gave some, apostles; and some, prophets; and some, evangelists; and some, pastors and teachers; Eph4:12 For the perfecting of the saints, for the work of the ministry, for the edifying of the body of Christ: KJV)*

# -8-

# The Apostolic Manifesto

*Eph 4:13 Till we all come in the unity of the faith, and of the knowledge of the Son of God, unto a perfect man, unto the measure of the stature of the fullness of Christ: (KJV)*

Apostles are charged with the responsibility of keeping The Church in alignment with the Word of God. God has set them in The Church as the first accountable relative to church alignment.

> *1Cr 12:28 And God hath set some in the church, first apostles, secondarily prophets, thirdly teachers, after that miracles, then gifts of healings, helps, governments, diversities of tongues. (KJV)*

Apostles are not installed by <u>anyone</u>, they are chosen by God, (Galatians 1:1).

Apostle Paul made it a point to correct, rebuke, and continuously align the people of God with the Word of God. Paul would start with The Church leaders, and worked his way through the whole congregation. Paul wanted to make sure that The Church stayed with sound doctrine. He warned The Church about being seduced by demonic and evil spirits and doctrine of demons.

# -8-

# The Apostolic Manifesto

>*1Ti 4:1 Now the Spirit speaketh expressly, that in the latter times some shall depart from the faith, giving heed to seducing spirits, and doctrines of devils; 1Ti 4:2 Speaking lies in hypocrisy; having their conscience seared with a hot iron; (KJV)*

The Apostle Paul understood very clearly that if The Church kept heading in the direction it was going, certain things would occur. Because he had *Apostolic Insight*, God revealed to him the consequences of disobedience.

>*2Ti 4:1 I charge [thee] therefore before God, and the Lord Jesus Christ, who shall judge the quick and the dead at his appearing and his kingdom; 2Ti 4:2 Preach the word; be instant in season, out of season; reprove, rebuke, exhort with all longsuffering and doctrine. 2Ti 4:3 For the time will come when they will not endure sound doctrine; but after their own lusts shall they heap to themselves teachers, having itching ears; (KJV)*

I want to restate first Timothy chapter four beginning in verse one. Because I wanted to emphasize the point relative to where The Church is now. It's a matter of record, if one cares to look and do the research.

# -8-

# The Apostolic Manifesto

*1Ti 4:1 Now the Spirit speaketh expressly, that in the latter times some shall depart from the faith, giving heed to seducing spirits, and doctrines of devils; 1Ti 4:2 Speaking lies in hypocrisy; having their conscience seared with a hot iron;(KJV)*

The Church to a great degree has embraced doctrines of demons; we have witches, warlocks, and wizards pastoring churches. You can view some "Christian Television", programs for examples of false demonic preaching. They call themselves the servants of God.  My question would be, which God?

The Apostle Paul stated that we would be living in very difficult times for The Church. We would be living in a time that will be totally wicked, self-centered, full of hate, and having a form of godliness. At the same time denying the power of the Holy Spirit, the Comforter and the Helper from God; that would keep The Church in alignment. Review the second book of Timothy, the third chapter beginning in verse one.

*2Ti 3:1This know also, that in the last days perilous times shall come.  2Ti 3:2 For men shall be lovers of their own selves, covetous, boasters, proud, blasphemers, disobedient to parents, unthankful, unholy, 2Ti 3:3 Without natural affection, trucebreakers, false accusers, incontinent, fierce, despisers of those that are good, (KJV)*

# -8-

# The Apostolic Manifesto

When one attends church or claims to belong to a Christian denomination and does not submit to the power of the Holy Spirit, then they are wasting their time and playing games with themselves. You look like a Christian on the outside, but on the inside you deny the power of God. A large part of The Church and the people who call themselves Christians are guilty of this.

> *2Ti 3:4 Traitors, heady, high minded, lovers of pleasures more than lovers of God; 2Ti 3:5 Having a form of godliness, but denying the power thereof: from such turn away. 2Ti 3:6 For of this sort are they which creep into houses, and lead captive silly women laden with sins, led away with divers lusts, 2Ti 3:7 Ever learning, and never able to come to the knowledge of the truth. 2Ti 3:8 Now as Jannes and Jambres withstood Moses, so do these also resist the truth: men of corrupt minds, reprobate concerning the faith. (KJV)*

That was a mentality that existed in Paul's society that found its way into The Church. Paul indicated that it was an attitude that had to be challenged and some will withstand the truth in The Church now, as they withstood Moses then.

Jesus Christ made it clear that as it was in Genesis the sixth chapter, so it will be at the end of this age. When you research the days of Noah, you will come to understand that it was a period of demonic wickedness. To the extent that God destroyed all but eight people.

# -8-

# The Apostolic Manifesto

> *Mat 24:37 "But as the days of Noah [were], so also will the coming of the Son of Man be. Mat 24:38 "For as in the days before the flood, they were eating and drinking, marrying and giving in marriage, until the day that Noah entered the ark, (NKJ)*

Jude had and has something to say about the state of believers which compose The Church. He warned about a state of mind relative to fallen angels (generators of evil spirits). There is a breaking down of Godly standards, first in the society and then in The Church.

> *Jud 1:6  And the angels which kept not their first estate, but left their own habitation, he hath reserved in everlasting chains under darkness unto the judgment of the great day. Jud 1:7  Even as Sodom and Gomorrha, and the cities about them in like manner, giving themselves over to fornication, and going after strange flesh, are set forth for an example, suffering the vengeance of eternal fire. (KJV)*

Those of us who see that we are living in a time of perversion and compromise within the Christian Church must respond. We must do what Enoch, Noah, Abraham, Moses, Joshua, Elisha, and Elijah did. We must stand up like true disciples of Jesus Christ. Moving with an Apostolic unction to restore holiness and righteousness to The Church of Jesus Christ.

# -8-

# The Apostolic Manifesto

The Triune God is moving, shifting, shaking, and rearranging. God has allowed things to occur in order to see who would manifest in the Apostolic. The Apostolic Manifesto has been written in the pages of the Holy Scripture, the Word of God. All those who claim to be Christians are responsible to carry it out. But leaders must lead the way. The Godly leaders must become manifest; God is watching every move.

Apostle Paul addresses the issue of manifest, in several texts in the first book of Corinthians. In several locations, he makes use of the term manifest.

> *1Cr 3:13 Every man's work shall be made manifest for the day shall declare it, because it shall be revealed by fire; and the fire shall try every man's work of what sort it is 1Cr 4:5 Therefore judge nothing before the time until the Lord come who both will bring to light the hidden things of darkness and will make manifest the counsels of the hearts and then shall every man have praise of God. 1Cr 11:19 For there must be also heresies among you that they which are approved may be made manifest among you. (KJV)*

Strong's Exhaustive Concordance, uses two Greek words to define manifest. *Phaneros*-G5318, *Phaneroō*-G5319, they are defined respectively.

# -8-

# The Apostolic Manifesto

*Phaneros*- G5318

> 1) apparent, manifest, evident, known.
>
> 2) manifest i.e. to be plainly recognized or known.

*Phaneroō*- G5319

> 1) to make manifest or visible or known what has been hidden or unknown, to manifest, whether by words, or deeds, or in any other way, a) make actual and visible, realized ,b) to make known by teaching, c) to become manifest, be made known, d) of a person.
>
> *1) expose to view, make manifest, to show one's self, appear, e) to become known, to be plainly recognized, thoroughly understood. (Strong's Exhaustive Concordance)*

It behooves all of us to pay attention to what the Word of God says. We need to spend more time in prayer, fasting and studying the Word of God. Assumptions, denominationalism, and self-righteous dismissal of sin will not satisfy the Triune God regime. Natural and supernatural forces from hell have already been unleashed, to bring down The Church and to destroy the Saints of God. God is shifting from His tolerance of unholy and unrighteous behavior. He is moving toward a Noah's flood mentality, with a Sodom and Gomorrah resolution. I am not trying to imply that

# -8-

# The Apostolic Manifesto

the whole Church has become polluted and leavened. But we know a little leaven, leavens the whole lump, Gal 5:9 *"A little leaven leavens the whole lump."* (NKJV)

God has already shifted. He is going to shake up The Church starting with the leadership. Those of us who are sadden with the abominations of Deuteronomy the eighteenth chapter; will not suffer the Ezekiel ninth chapter judgment.

> *Deu18:9-14[9] When thou art come into the land which the LORD thy God giveth thee, thou shalt not learn to do after the abominations of those nations. [10] There shall not be found among you [any one] that maketh his son or his daughter to pass through the fire,[or] that useth divination, [or] an observer of times, or an enchanter, or a witch, [11] Or a charmer, or a consulter with familiar spirits, or a wizard, or a necromancer. [12] For all that do these things [are] an abomination unto the LORD: and because of these abominations the LORD thy God doth drive them out from before thee. [13] Thou shalt be perfect with the LORD thy God. [14] For these nations, which thou shalt possess, hearkened unto observers of times, and unto diviners: but as for thee, the LORD thy God hath not suffered thee so [to do]. (KJV)*

## -8-

# The Apostolic Manifesto

Notice the supernatural activity that is taking place relative to the servants of God. Focus on what God says to His servant Ezekiel. Notice the criteria in which leaders are evaluated, relative to righteousness and judgment. Notice the term abomination and the criteria God uses to determine the proper attitude.

> *Eze 9:4-7 [4] and the LORD said to him, "Go through the midst of the city, through the midst of Jerusalem, and put a mark on the foreheads of the men who sigh and cry over all the abominations that are done within it." [5] To the others He said in my hearing, "Go after him through the city and kill; do not let your eye spare, nor have any pity. [6] "Utterly slay old [and] young men, maidens and little children and women; but do not come near anyone on whom [is] the mark; and begin at My sanctuary." So they began with the elders who [were] before the temple. [7] Then He said to them, "Defile the temple, and fill the courts with the slain. Go out!" And they went out and killed in the city. (NKJV)*

Do we dare risk this level of judgment, because we compromised the Word of God for political correctness? I speak to leaders of churches, para church organizations, ministries and collaborations. I speak to all who claim Jesus Christ as Lord and Savior. I suggest a thorough reading and study of Deuteronomy, the eighteenth chapter and Ezekiel, the ninth chapter.

# -8-

# The Apostolic Manifesto

Please don't get this twisted, God is speaking to _you and your_ Church; and to everyone who is and claims to be a servant of Jesus Christ of Nazareth. There is a point where if the chosen refused to obey, they will be frozen in what **they have chosen.**

> **Rev 22:11 He that is unjust, let him be unjust still: and he which is filthy, let him be filthy still: and he that is righteous, let him be righteous still: and he that is holy, let him be holy still. (KJV)**

God is in "God Shift Mode", which means that The Church must shift or get left behind this includes everyone.

# Apostolic Manifesto

# -9-

# The God Shift

## The Number Thirteen (13)

Many have bought the lie that the number thirteen is purely evil and a sign of rebellion. There were twelve disciples, but Jesus the Christ made the thirteenth participant at the Last Supper. Judas rebelled against his assignment not Jesus. In Fact, the Bible has many examples of both good and evil, relative to the number thirteen. Because of time and space we will only cite a few positive examples.

I believe that the enemy Satan has deceived most of the world and The Church to react negatively relative to the number thirteen. I believe and will prove from the Word of God that the number thirteen holds a "Breakthrough Revelation" for the body of Christ in 2013.

> *"In Genesis 16:15-17 it reveals that when "Hagar bore Ishmael, Abraham was 86 years old." Then "when Abraham was 99 years old the Lord appeared to him" and iterated the Promise again---that He will give Abraham a son by his wife. I will bless her, and she will produce nations; kings of peoples will come from her."(See Genesis17:1-22)*

> *At 99 years old, God's Promise came. At 86 years old, Abraham tried to bring about God's Promise. 13 years between the Promise given*

# -9-

# The God Shift

*and the Promise manifested. Therefore, 99 minus 86 equals 13. This is "The Number 13 Promise". The Number 13 Promise is a "two-fold" promise. It always involves man and it always involves God. It always has seasons, times and circumstances in which God and man participate." (Number 13 Meaning)*

I want to make a point here. I know the "Holy Bible" was not written in chapter and verse break down. But for the purpose of study and easy reference, it was translated that way. I do find it interesting that the way verses break down or break up has revelation.

## God Uses Thirteen When Transitioning Man

### *Abraham*

*In Genesis 13:1-4 Gen 13:1, "And Abram went up out of Egypt, he, and his wife, and all that he had, and Lot with him, into the south. Gen. 13:2, And Abram [was] very rich in cattle, in silver, and in gold. Gen.13:3 And he went on his journeys from the south even to Bethel, unto the place where his tent had been at the beginning, between Bethel and Hai; Gen. 13:4 Unto the place of the altar, which he had made there at the first: and there Abram called on the name of the LORD."(KJV)*

# -9-

# The God Shift

## Moses

*Exodus 13:1-3, "And the LORD spake unto Moses, saying, Exd.13:2, Sanctify unto me all the firstborn, whatsoever openeth the womb among the children of Israel, [both] of man and of beast: it [is] mine. Exd. 13:3, And Moses said unto the people, Remember this day, in which ye came out from Egypt, out of the house of bondage; for by strength of hand the LORD brought you out from this [place]: there shall no leavened bread be eaten."(KJV)*

## Joshua

*Joshua 6:15 "And it came to pass on the seventh day, that they rose early about the dawning of the day, and compassed the city after the same manner seven times: only on that day they compassed the city seven times." Jos. 6:20, "So the people shouted when [the priests] blew with the trumpets: and it came to pass, when the people heard the sound of the trumpet, and the people shouted with a great shout, that the wall fell down flat, so that the people went up into the city, every man straight before him, and they took the city." (KJV)*

They marched around the walls "Thirteen Times", in total. If you want to argue original Bible structure, you still have to deal with content, relative to context.

# -9-

# The God Shift

## God Uses Thirteen In World Transformation

### Apostle Paul

Paul was the true thirteenth Apostle; his first missionary mission was started in A.D. 47. Paul was "arrested" by Jesus in A.D. 34. Thirteen years later he went on his first missionary journey. Rom 11:13; **"For I speak to you Gentiles, In as much as I am the apostle of the Gentiles."**(KJV)

God used Paul to change the paradigm from Jews exclusively to all people relative to salvation, (Acts 22:21).

### The Thirteenth Tribe of Revelation Seven

Last, but not denied, the "Thirteenth Tribe" of Rev.7:9, what is revealed here cannot be explained away as coincidence or book of "Revelation" end time poetry.

> *Rev.7:9"After this I beheld, and, lo, a great multitude, which no man could number, of all nations, and kindreds, and people, and tongues, stood before the throne, and before the Lamb, clothed with white robes, and palms in their hands." (KJV)*

# -9-

# The God Shift

*Rev 7:13, "And one of the elders answered, saying unto me, What are these which are arrayed in white robes? and whence came they?  Rev 7:14 And I said unto him, Sir, thou knowest. And he said to me, These are they which came out of great tribulation, and have washed their robes, and made them white in the blood of the Lamb. Rev7:15 Therefore are they before the throne of God, and serve him day and night in his temple: and he that sitteth on the throne shall dwell among them."(KJV)*

When you examine what God gave in Revelation the seventh chapter something stands out. God selected twelve thousand from each of the twelve tribes of Israel, but the "Thirteenth Spiritual Tribe" of all nations could not be numbered. Again God manifested in the number thirteen, in a way that cannot be denied.

At this point I need to clear up a few things. I do not **believe in numerology**, but I do believe God uses numbers. I know the Devil, Satan, and all of his cohorts want us to be confused about the number thirteen. Biblical numbers have meaning and we need to recognize what it meant coming out of the year 2012, and what it means going into the year 2013 and beyond. I have just scratched the surface.

# -9-

# The God Shift

Some may still want to argue that the Bible is not written in chapters and in verses and you would be correct. But it still doesn't mean that the significance of the events centered around the number thirteen are not valid. You may want to call it coincidence, of course that is your right and privilege.

## The Number Thirteen Promise

1. **The promise is always initiated by God and destined to change the world forever.**

2. **Concerning man, to obtain the promise is beyond hope-impossible!**

3. **Concerning God, the chosen opportunity to manifest His plan of blessing and change. (Number 13 Meaning)**

## Three Conditions Of The Church

I have been involved in organizational design, training facilitation, organizational strategy implementation, program evaluation and program development in the secular arena for over thirty years. I've been involved with church organizations for more than forty years; as a so-called layperson and leader. I've been a Deacon, Minister, Elder, Pastor, Consultant, and have operated at the Apostolic level of service to the Body of Christ. I understand church dynamics, politics and church nonsense.

# -9-

# The God Shift

My responsibilities have been latrine captain, usher, youth educational coordinator, youth athletic coordinator, social activity committee coordinator, as well as teacher and preacher. I am also well trained in how to receive abuse and how to tolerate being dehumanized. I have six earned degrees: three Doctorates, two Masters and a Bachelor's degree. This is from a foundation of basically a sixth grade education and a GED. Again, I have over thirty years of experience in the secular arena relative to organizational strategy, implementation and training. I specialize in assessment, evaluation and recommendations. Based on the Holy Spirit and my experience in dynamic engagement; my assessment of The Church condition is explained in three models. The three models are "Confusion-Conflict", "Antichrist", and "Christ Alignment."

## *Confusion-Conflict Model*

The "Confusion-Conflict Model", (Figure1 p. 94), is a condition where leadership is compromised and the focus is: more revenue, political correctness, power and control, and society dictated morals. Decisions in this model are only partially made based on the Holy Scripture. The Saints are polarized and there is a great deal of competition for the pastor's attention among men and women. There is usually a permissiveness based on a "Counterfeit Grace", a grace that allows sin in order to get grace. Depending on what denomination is under review, the size of the donation will usually dictate the size and amount of the sins you are allowed to commit.

# -9-

# The God Shift

The "Confusion-Conflict Model" represents an unaligned church. The fundamental characteristic of the relatively unaligned church team is wasted energy and efforts. The leadership and the membership of The Church may be hard workers, but there's conflict and confusion about who is in charge. Individuals may work extraordinarily hard, but their efforts do not efficiently translate to a Godly team effort. There is a belief in God, but compromise is a problem. Empowering individuals in this model increases confusion and the likelihood is that the Word of God will be compromised. Low levels of alignment worsens the chaos and makes managing The Church more difficult.

"A little leaven leavens the whole lump", and when a/The Church will not deal with leaven (sin), it's a setup for destruction. This will lead to the Antichrist Model, and the eventual dissolving of a congregation.

> **1Cr5:6 Your glorying [is] not good. Know ye not that a little leaven leaveneth the whole lump? 1Cr 5:7 Purge out therefore the old leaven, that ye may be a new lump, as ye are unleavened. For even Christ our Passover is sacrificed for us: 1Cr 5:8 Therefore let us keep the feast, not with old leaven, neither with the leaven of malice and wickedness; but with the unleavened [bread] of sincerity and truth. (KJV)**

When heresy is tolerated in The Church, whether it be the preaching, teaching, prophet-lying, oh I meant to say is prophesying. In this condition decline is inevitable. We

92

# -9-

# The God Shift

cannot tolerate a contamination of the Word of God, under any circumstances. Corruption of the Word must be stopped.

> *Gal 1:6 I marvel that ye are so soon removed from him that called you into the grace of Christ unto another gospel: Gal 1:7 Which is not another; but there be some that trouble you, and would pervert the gospel of Christ. Gal 1:8 But though we, or an angel from heaven, preach any other gospel unto you than that which we have preached unto you, let him be accursed. Gal 1:9 As we said before, so say I now again, If any [man] preach any other gospel unto you than that ye have received, let him be accursed. Gal 5:9 A little leaven leaveneth the whole lump. (KJV)*

# -9-

# The God Shift

## Figure 1- Confusion-Conflict Model

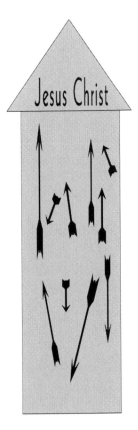

**The Arrows Represent**
**Churches-Pastors**
**Five Fold Ministries-Board Members-Membership**

# -9-

# The God Shift

## *Antichrist Model*

The" Antichrist Model", (Figure 2 p.99), reflects a church condition that is in total chaos. It has become a place of warring factions and promiscuity, relative to the Word of God. The truth is being totally compromised and instead of the "Church Leaders" setting the example of Godliness, they are the best examples of wretched behavior. There is bickering and fighting and every level of sin.

This is what happens in church when issues are not dealt with in the Confusion-Conflict phase. The end results and consequences of this model is that The Church splits multiple times and/or ceases to exist completely. Revenue is usually misappropriated and women and children are abused without retribution. Let me make myself clear, women and children are sexually abused. There is adultery, fornication, sodomy as well as psychological and physiological abuse. In most cases, all pretense of Holiness has been abandoned.

Individuals who want to maintain personal righteousness are leaving in droves: some find other churches, some have stopped going to church altogether and others turn away from God. People are distraught because they can't believe that God let this happen. The wolves are consuming the flock from

# -9-

# The God Shift

within. People are psychologically damaged and faith in God is almost destroyed.

You may be aware of such a condition; if you are, what are you doing about it? Spiritual lives are at stake. We have a responsibility to pray, fast and be personally accountable to the Word of God. The Antichrist Model is created by the Antichrist Spirit. This is the primary spirit that blocks the Word of God and fights against the Holy Spirit.

> *1Jo 2:18, Little children, it is the last time: and as ye have heard that antichrist shall come, even now are there many antichrists; whereby we know that it is the last time.1Jo 2:22 Who is a liar but he that denieth that Jesus is the Christ? He is antichrist, that denieth the Father and the Son. 1Jo 4:3 And every spirit that confesseth not that Jesus Christ is come in the flesh is not of God: and this is that [spirit] of antichrist, whereof ye have heard that it should come; and even now already is it in the world. 2Jo 1:7 For many deceivers are entered into the world, who confess not that Jesus Christ is come in the flesh. This is a deceiver and an antichrist. (KJV)*

The Antichrist Spirit has found its way into The Church. It is eating away at it like a cancer would eat away at a human body. The only treatment is back to Holiness, Righteousness and a Commitment to speak up

# -9-

# The God Shift

for the truth. True servants of God must become Manifest, before the whole lump, (The Church and Your church), becomes leavened.

A wait-and-see attitude is destructive, disobedient, stubborn, rebellious and cowardly. Too much of The Church looks like the Antichrist Model, or worse, today. We all need to go to God the Father in prayer seeking direction and correction. We are going to have to be proactive and willing to conduct ourselves relative to the instructions in Mathew the eighteenth chapter.

> *Mat 18:15 Moreover if thy brother shall trespass against thee, go and tell him his fault between thee and him alone: if he shall hear thee, thou hast gained thy brother. Mat 18:16 But if he will not hear [thee, then] take with thee one or two more, that in the mouth of two or three witnesses every word may be established. Mat 18:17 And if he shall neglect to hear them, tell [it] unto the church: but if he neglect to hear the church, let him be unto thee as an heathen man and a publican. (KJV)*

Clearly a decision must be made if The Church is going to avoid the "Antichrist Model." It is decision time or destruction time, you choose.

# -9-

# The God Shift

*Deu 30:15 See, I have set before thee this day life and good, and death and evil; Deu 30:19 I call heaven and earth to record this day against you, [that] I have set before you life and death, blessing and cursing: therefore choose life, that both thou and thy seed may live: Rev 22:11 He that is unjust, let him be unjust still: and he which is filthy, let him be filthy still: and he that is righteous, let him be righteous still: and he that is holy, let him be holy still, (KJV)*

# -9-

# The God Shift

## Figure 2- Antichrist Model

**The Arrows Represent
Churches-Pastors
Five Fold Ministries-Board Members-Membership**

# -9-

# The God Shift

## *Christ Alignment Model*

The "Christ Alignment Model", (Figure 3 p.102), should be the goal for every church, and ministry. This model can only be accomplished through obedience and dedication to Holiness, Wholeness, and Oneness with God the Father, Jesus Christ, and the Holy Spirit. This must be an internal process that is manifested externally, having a form of Godliness will not pass the test of the "Kingdom of God" examination.

> *Mat 6:33 But seek ye first the kingdom of God, and his righteousness; and all these things shall be added unto you. Mat 5:48 Be ye therefore perfect, even as your Father which is in heaven is perfect. (KJV)*

It goes without saying that this model is the one that God will bless and show favor. This model cannot be attained without operating in the Holy Spirit and in Truth. The focus of worship in this model is concentrated on the Holy Spirit and Truth. God the Father is searching the earth for a group of servants that exemplify the" Christ Alignment Model."

> *Jhn 4:23 But the hour cometh, and now is, when the true worshippers shall worship the Father in spirit and in truth: for the Father seeketh such to worship him. Jhn 4:24 God [is] a Spirit: and they that worship him must worship [him] in spirit and in truth. (KJV)*

# -9-

# The God Shift

This church model is not a model without problems. Anywhere you have people grouped together, you are going to have problems. The difference is that the leadership deals with problems in a Godly manner, people are led to Christ rather than men. The Word of God is preached no matter the political climate. The leadership and the membership are concerned with Theocracy, and not religious theology. People are striving to overcome their sins and not hide under "Fake Grace", which is counterfeit and demonic at its core.

> *Rom 6:1 What shall we say then? Shall we continue in sin, that grace may abound? Rom 6:2 God forbid. How shall we, that are dead to sin, live any longer therein? Rom 6:3 Know ye not, that so many of us as were baptized into Jesus Christ were baptized into his death? Rom 6:4 Therefore we are buried with him by baptism into death: that like as Christ was raised up from the dead by the glory of the Father, even so we also should walk in newness of life. (KJV)*

> *Rom 5:21 That as sin hath reigned unto death, even so might grace reign through righteousness unto eternal life by Jesus Christ our Lord. (KJV)*

# -9-

# The God Shift

## Figure 3- Christ Alignment Model

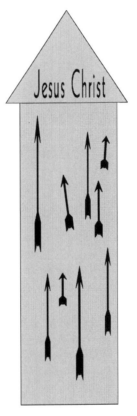

**The Arrows Represent
Churches-Pastors
Five Fold Ministries-Board Members-Membership**

# -9-

# The God Shift

## *Summary*

The three models have been presented and I believe they represent the condition of The Church and ministries. The three models or conditions can all exist at the same time, in the same church or ministry, or at any given point in time. We must be willing as the "Five Fold" ministries and other ministry gifts to stand up for the true Word of God. Holiness and Righteousness are not negotiable terms relative to the Kingdom of God. False, fake, religious, and Satanic grace has to be shut down. We must operate in legitimacy and not illegitimately relative to the treatment of "Kingdom of God" issues. God has issued a call to order, will we heed?

To move forward it will take the "Holy Spirit", legitimate Apostolic courage, vision, insight and a willingness to suffer for the Kingdom of God. The Triune God regime has prepared a people for service, and they will become manifest.

> *1Cr 11:18 For first of all, when ye come together in the church, I hear that there be divisions among you; and I partly believe it. 1Cr 11:19 For there must be also heresies among you, that they which are approved may be made manifest among you. (KJ V)*

# Apostolic Manifesto

# -10-

# The Manifesto

# A Call To Order

1. The Ten Commandments must be viewed based on the directives made by Jesus Christ.

> *Mat 5:17 Think not that I am come to destroy the law, or the prophets: I am not come to destroy, but to fulfil. Mat 5:18 For verily I say unto you, Till heaven and earth pass, one jot or one tittle shall in no wise pass from the law, till all be fulfilled. (KJV)*

2. We must return to Holiness relative to the Word of God.

> *Psa 29:2 Give unto the LORD the glory due unto his name; worship the LORD in the beauty of holiness. 1Th 4:7 For God hath not called us unto uncleanness, but unto holiness. 1Th 4:8 He therefore that despiseth, not man, but God, who hath also given unto us his Holy Spirit. Rom 6:22 But now being made free from sin, and become servants to God, ye have your fruit unto holiness, and the end everlasting life. Hbr 12:14 Follow peace with all [men], and holiness, without which no man shall see the Lord: (KJV)*

# -10-

# The Manifesto

# A Call To Order

3.    The Kingdom of God and His total pure righteousness must be the focus, the first priority. The perfection of His great agenda cannot be questioned.

> *Mat 6:33 But seek ye first the kingdom of God, and his righteousness; and all these things shall be added unto you. Mat 6:34Take therefore no thought for the morrow: for the morrow shall take thought for the things of itself. Sufficient unto the day [is] the evil thereof. Mat 5:48 Be ye therefore perfect, even as your Father which is in heaven is perfect. (KJV)*

4.    Those of us who are in leadership must be willing to point out sin in The Church and not conform to the dictates of this society in rebellion to the Word of God.

> *Isa 58:1 Cry aloud, spare not, lift up thy like a trumpet, and shew my people their transgression, and the house of Jacob their sins. (KJV)*

# -10-

# The Manifesto

# A Call To Order

*Rom 12:1 I beseech you therefore, brethren, by the mercies of God, that ye present your bodies a living sacrifice, holy, acceptable unto God, [which is] your reasonable service. Rom 12:2 And be not conformed to this world: but be ye transformed by the renewing of your mind, that ye may prove what [is] that good, and acceptable, and perfect, will of God. (KJV)*

5.     The leaders of The Church must stop ordaining individuals, because they can play an instrument, are good orators, hold a high position in secular industry, and/or have a great deal of resources and revenue they can bring to The Church.

*1Ti 5:22 Lay hands suddenly on no man, neither be partaker of other men's sins: keep thyself pure. (KJV)*

6.     There must be accountability in The Church. We must stop covering up sin in The Church among those in leadership, as well as those who are not.

# -10-

# The Manifesto

# A Call To Order

*1Ti5:19 Against an elder receive not an accusation, but before two or three witnesses. 1Ti 5:20 Them that sin rebuke before all, that others also may fear. 1Ti 5:21 I charge [thee] before God, and the Lord Jesus Christ, and the elect angels, that thou observe these things without preferring one before another, doing nothing by partiality. (KJV)*

*Mat 18:15 Moreover if thy brother shall trespass against thee, go and tell him his fault between thee and him alone: if he shall hear thee, thou hast gained thy brother. Mat 18:16 But if he will not hear [thee, then] take with thee one or two more, that in the mouth of two or three witnesses every word may be established. Mat 18:17 And if he shall neglect to hear them, tell [it] unto the church: but if he neglect to hear the church, let him be unto thee as an heathen man and a publican. (KJV)*

7.    We must manifest the power of God's Love to the whole world. Because of obedience to and for the love of His Word; as well as a love for one another.

*Jhn 3:16 For God so loved the world, that he gave his only begotten Son, that whosoever believeth in him should not perish, but have everlasting life. Jhn 14:23 Jesus answered and said unto him, If a man love me, he will keep my words: and my Father will love him, and we will come unto*

# -10-

# The Manifesto

# A Call To Order

*him, and make our abode with him. Jhn 14:24 He that loveth me not keepeth not my sayings: and the word which ye hear is not mine, but the Father's which sent me. 1Jo 4:7 Beloved, let us love one another: for love is of God; and every one that loveth is born of God, and knoweth God. 1Jo 4:8 He that loveth not knoweth not God; for God is love. (KJV)*

8.     The Church of God must get its economic, and legal matters in order, so it can manage the wealth that The Lord Jesus Christ wants to pour into it.

*1Cr 14:40 Let all things be done decently and in order. Rom 13:6 For this cause pay ye tribute also: for they are God's ministers, attending continually upon this very thing. Rom13:7 Render therefore to all their dues: tribute to whom tribute [is due]; custom to whom custom; fear to whom fear; honour to whom honour. Mat 25:27 Thou oughtest therefore to have put my money to the exchangers, and [then] at my coming I should have received mine own with usury. (KJV)*

# -10-

# The Manifesto

# A Call To Order

9. The Church of God must stop ignoring the demonic intrusions into The Church, (1Tim.4:1, NKJV). We must stop pretending that witches, warlocks and spell casters do not exist in The Church. We have a directive to put witches and the like out of the body, (Deut. 13). Part of the great commission of "The Church of God", is casting out demons.

> *Mar 16:17 And these signs shall follow them that believe; In my name shall they cast out devils; they shall speak with new tongues; Mar 16:18 They shall take up serpents; and if they drink any deadly thing, it shall not hurt them; they shall lay hands on the sick, and they shall recover. 1Ti 4:1 Now the Spirit speaketh expressly, that in the latter times some shall depart from the faith, giving heed to seducing spirits, and doctrines of devils; 1Ti 4:2 Speaking lies in hypocrisy; having their conscience seared with a hot iron; (KJV)*

10. The Church must take action. The Church must be proactive and not passive. We be must doers of the Word of God, just not listeners and spectators.

> **Jam 1:22 But be ye doers of the word, and not hearers only, deceiving your own selves. Jam 2:26 For as the body without the spirit is dead, so faith without works is dead also.** *(KJV)*

# -10-

# The Manifesto

# A Call To Order

Churches, ministries, church/ministry collaborators, individuals operating in what has been called fivefold ministry should take heed. We are in an Apostolic countdown. As Martin Luther nailed his Reformation on the door of The Church; I'm nailing this "Apostolic Manifesto, A Call To Order", on the door of The Church of today. Too many churches are out of order and out of alignment with the Word of God. Whether you agree or disagree, I know that you are thinking about it, talking about it, and some of you will actually do something about it.

For those of you who are already ahead of the curve, may the true God of Heaven legitimize you, bless you and keep you. For those of you who have been inspired to make some changes, may God give you the courage. For those of you who decide to do nothing, then you've already abdicated your Kingdom Blessing. Your Kingdom Blessing will be equal to your Kingdom Investment.

> *Gal 6:7 Be not deceived; God is not mocked: for whatsoever a man soweth, that shall he also reap. Gal 6:8 For he that soweth to his flesh shall of the flesh reap corruption; but he that soweth to the Spirit shall of the Spirit reap life everlasting. (KJV)*

# References

Frangipane, Francis. (1989). *The three battlefields.* Cedar Rapids, Iowa: Arrow Publications.

Hislop, Alexander (1919/1998). *The two Babylons.* Ontario, California: Chick Publications.

http://www.Dictionary.com 2013

http://www.merriam-webster.com/dictionary/apostle

http://www.references.com 2013

Mitchell, L. D. (1999). *Liberty in Jesus.* Durham, England: The Pentland Press.

Murphy, Dr. Edward (1996). *The handbook for spiritual warfare.* Nashville: Thomas Nelson Publishers,

*"Number 13 Meaning, It's a Powerful Blessing From God".* Stephen Gola (2008). http://www.faithwriters.com/article-details.php?id=82702

Rutz, James H., (2005). *Megashift.* Colorado Springs, Colorado: Empowerment Press

*Strong's Exhaustive Concordance,* http://www.blueletterbible.org

# References

*"The Conversion of Constantine"*,
http://www.religionfacts.com/christianity/history/constantine.htm

*"The Motivation and Mystery of Godly Behavior"*.
http://www.biblegateway.com/resources/ivp-nt/Motivation-Mystery-Godly

*The New Apostolic Churches*, C. Peter Wagner, Ed. Ventura, California: Regal, 1998. Elmer L. Towns.

*The New Apostolic Churches*, C. Peter Wagner, Ed. Ventura, California: Regal, 1998. John Eckhart.

*"Willie Lynch Letter: The Making of a Slave"*, Final Call.com News,http://www.finalcall.com/artman/publish/Perspectives_1/Willie_Lynch_letter_The_Making_of_a_Slave.shtml

*"Why Holy Ghost?"* Donald Reagan,
http://www.learnthebible.org/why-holy-ghost.html.

*"Why the King James Version CANNOT be the ONLY TRUE "inspired version" of God's Word"*. Carl Gallop. *http://www.hickoryhammockbaptist.org.*

Wink, W. (1992). *Engaging the powers: discernment and resistance in a world of domination.* Minneapolis: Fortress Press.

Wylie-Kellermann, B. (1991). *Season of faith and conscience: Kairos, confessilitrugy.* Maryknoll, NY: Orbis.

# Apostolic Manifesto

# Appendix A

## High-Tech Willie Lynch(ing) Crucifixion

First of all I must warn you if you're willing to tell the truth, be prepared to be attacked by demonic personalities led by so-called Christians Leaders, who have an agenda or who are deceived or both. This year I was giving a presentation titled "Origins and Counterfeits" that addressed issues that some could say are controversial. This was supposedly a spiritual warfare environment and I addressed issues of spiritual warfare relative to demonology, disembodied spirits, Adam and Eve, and Cain and Abel.

I also addressed the illegitimacy of Cain relative to Adam and the fact that there were two Enoch's. One Enoch was the son of Cain, of Genesis the fourth chapter. The other Enoch was the son of Jared, of Genesis the fifth chapter. Enoch, the son of Jared, is the one Jude quoted in the book of Jude. My presentation basically pointed out that Satan was the first religious Theological Entity, and that God the Father is the original Theocrat.

During this presentation I made a statement that I would entertain questions, questions mind you not challenges, debates or arguments. Evidently there was an individual in the group who took exception to my presentation who had a demonic religious slant, who became argumentative. It was obvious to most of the individuals present that this individual had a demonic problem. I realized my mistake and shut the dialogue down to avoid disintegration of the process.

# Appendix A

## High-Tech Willie Lynch(ing) Crucifixion

Near the end of my presentation I could see the individual who had tried to interrupt my presentation, jumping up and down at the rear of the room. His arms were raised as though he had won a championship fight. I refused to be distracted and continued closing with a mass deliverance prayer.

It is important to point out at this time, that there were three African-American males in the meeting that involved about one hundred participants. The light-skinned African-American male walked up to the speakers area and began to criticize what I had said, from the perspective that I did not allow questions. Now let me remind you, the individual that I shut down did not have a question but wanted to argue and debate. The light-skinned African-American male proceeded to bring the Caucasian male up and gave him permission to attack, dehumanize, disrespect, make false statements about what I had said as well as threaten me.

I knew the person who led the attack,(the light-skinned African-American male), at least I thought I did. I began to feel like a dark skin African-American male who was a field slave about to be Lynched-Crucified, led by a light skinned house slave, using a white male as point man. I maintained a Godly temperament so I could let the Holy Spirit give me Revelation. Some Caucasians Christians offered help, stating their disbelief for what was happening.

Some of you may question why I reference this incident the way I did, it is because I want to point out a demonic force that has crept into The Church. I call it the "*Willie Lynch Syndrome.*" According to documented research a slave owner

117

# Appendix A

## High-Tech Willie Lynch(ing) Crucifixion

by the name of Willie Lynch on December 25, 1712, outlined in a speech how to keep and maintain control over slaves. This was later published in a letter.

> *Gentlemen, you know what your problems are; I do not need to elaborate. I am not here to enumerate your problems, I am here to introduce you to a method of solving them. In my bag here, I have a foolproof method for controlling your black slaves. I guarantee every one of you that if installed correctly it will control the slaves for at least 300 years [2012]. My method is simple. Any member of your family or your overseer can use it. I have outlined a number of differences among the slaves and make the differences bigger. I use fear, distrust and envy for control.*

> *These methods have worked on my modest plantation in the West Indies and it will work throughout the South. Take this simple little list of differences and think about them. On top of my list is "age" but it's there only because it starts with an "A." The second is "COLOR" or shade, there is intelligence, size, sex, size of plantations and status on plantations, attitude of owners, whether the slaves live in the valley, on a hill, East, West, North, South, have fine hair, course hair, or is tall or short. Now that you have a list of differences, I shall give you an outline of action, but before that, I shall assure you that distrust is stronger than trust and envy stronger than adulation, respect or admiration. The Black slaves after receiving this indoctrination shall carry on and will become self-refueling and self-generating for hundreds of years, maybe thousands. Don't forget you must pitch the old black Male vs. the young black Male, and the young black Male against the old black male.*

# Appendix A

## High-Tech Willie Lynch(ing) Crucifixion

*You must use the dark skin slaves vs. the light skin slaves, and the light skin slaves vs. the dark skin slaves. You must use the female vs. the male. And the male vs. the female. You must also have you white servants and overseers distrust all Blacks. It is necessary that your slaves trust and depend on us. They must love, respect and trust only us. Gentlemen, these kits are your keys to control. Use them. Have your wives and children use them, never miss an opportunity. If used intensely for one year, the slaves themselves will remain perpetually distrustful of each other. (Willie Lynch Letter: The Making of a Slave)*

Based on several experiences, but especially this one particular event, I believe that the Willie Lynch syndrome has invaded The Church. In others words divide and conquer relative to every demographic, topology, gender and ethnicity possible. I believe that Satan is the biggest slave owner with the biggest plantation that ever existed. I believe that the strategies Willie Lynch received came directly from Satanic influences; since slavery and oppression is Satan's business.

*2Ti 2:26 and [that] they may come to their senses [and escape] the snare of the devil, having been taken captive by him to [do] his will. (NKJV)*

Some have stated that the Willie Lynch letter is a myth, some have also stated that Satan is a myth. Gravity still has an impact on our lives and is not based on our belief. I recommend the reading of the Willie Lynch letter to get a full understanding of the diabolical intent and ramifications.

# Appendix A

## High-Tech Willie Lynch(ing) Crucifixion

Whether the letter was written in 1712 or 2012, Satan's message is making a mark on The Church, in 2013 and beyond. This is not a black and white issue, this is not a tall and short issue, this is not a gender issue and this is not an issue of rich and poor. This is an issue of Satanic dehumanization, and the robbing, murdering, and the destruction of mankind. We who are "Kingdom of God" caretakers need to be aware of all of Satan's devices.

> *Jhn 10:10 The thief cometh not, but for to steal, and to kill, and to destroy: I am come that they might have life, and that they might have [it] more abundantly.  2 Cr 2:11  Lest Satan should get an advantage of us: for we are not ignorant of his devices. (KJV)*

# Appendix B

## Short Biography

Dr. Maddox has served God for over forty four years, and has been a leader in Youth Ministry, Radio Ministry, Satellite/TV (Total Christian Television) Leadership Training Ministry, and Inner Healing - Prayer and Deliverance Ministry. Dr. Maddox has served as a Deacon, Minister, and Elder. Dr. Maddox is currently the Pastor of the P.O.I.N.T.E. of Light Christian Center, which Jesus Christ led him to establish. Dr. Maddox is known nationally as a trainer, motivational speaker, and man of God in religious and secular arenas. Dr. Maddox is also President of Dr. E. Maddox Ministries. Dr. Maddox was called to be an Apostle by Jesus Christ, and this was confirmed by three men who are also Apostles.

Dr. Maddox has seen the power of God to save and deliver. God called him from a life of gang banging and drug dealing, to a life focused on helping others. God took a young man, with little more than a sixth grade education, and led him through a process from GED to Ph.D., and beyond. Dr. Maddox has earned these degrees, Bachelor of Science, Master of Arts/Business, Master of Public Administration, Doctor of Philosophy, Doctor of Ministry and Doctor of Education. Dr. Maddox has served as Dean of the Graduate Schools of Mission Leadership and Pastoral Leadership, at Destiny University in Ghana, Africa, and also served as an instructor at Power of the Word Bible College, Detroit MI. Dr. Maddox has served and taught the Word of God internationally in South Africa and Nigeria.

Dr. Maddox began his walk relative to Inner Healing and Deliverance Minis try over f o r t y years ago. He was involved in a very conservative church organization from 1969 until 2000. What Jesus Christ was revealing to him was viewed as taboo in that environment. As a result Dr. Maddox had to rely on God the Father, Jesus Christ, the Holy Spirit and his wife, of over thirty seven years, Barbara.

"Apostolic Manifesto", is a Word for You and Your Church, a "Call to Order. Dr. Maddox is available for consulting, training, teaching and preaching in all areas of ministry. Thank you for purchasing this book.

"His Kingdom Come; Amen"

Apostolic Manifesto

34033691R00083

Made in the USA
Charleston, SC
29 September 2014